Praise for *Power Referrals*

"*Power Referrals* will provide you with a road map to play the game with the intent to win!"

—Dr. Denis Waitley, bestselling author of *The Psychology of Winning*

"I am a firm believer in the concept of Ambassadors—I call them Apostles; Ken Blanchard calls them Raving Fans—as the ultimate customer business partner. Ambassadors are customer advocates spreading the all-important positive word-of-mouth goodwill in the marketplace for you, your products, and your business. They are invaluable—priceless! Andrea Sittig-Rolf's new book will unquestionably help you win more Ambassadors, which will give you an edge on your competition and substantially increase your sales and profits."

—Dr. Tony Alessandra, author of *The Platinum Rule*

"Andrea Sittig-Rolf doesn't just explain the concept and power of having Ambassadors in your life. She shows you how to go about identifying, connecting with, and appreciating them. Follow her strategies and you'll soon find both your personal and business lives improving exponentially."

—Tom Hopkins, world-renowned sales trainer and author of *How to Master the Art of Selling*

"Wow, Andrea nailed it! Relationships and networking are so vitally important to our success, and her insights are relevant, practical, and so true in today's sales world. *Power Referrals* is the secret sauce to achieving your next level of sales success!"

—Michael Norton, chairman and founder of Can-DoGo.com and president of Zig Ziglar Corporation

POWER
REFERRALS

Date: 01/27/12

658.8 SIT
Sittig-Rolf, Andrea.
Power referrals : the
ambassador method for

POWER
REFERRALS

The Ambassador Method for
Empowering Others to Promote Your Business
and Do the Selling for You

ANDREA SITTIG-ROLF

New York | Chicago | San Francisco | Lisbon | London
Madrid | Mexico City | Milan | New Delhi
San Juan | Seoul | Singapore | Sydney | Toronto

1 2 3 4 5 6 7 8 9 0   DOC/DOC   0 1 0 9 8

ISBN 978–0–07–159768–5
MHID 0–07–159768–9

McGraw-Hill books are available at special quantity discounts to use as premiums and sales promotions, or for use in corporate training programs. To contact a representative, please visit the Contact Us pages at www.mhprofessional.com.

This book is printed on acid-free paper.

The Blitz Experience® is a registered trademark of Andrea Sittig-Rolf.

For my husband, Brian Rolf, my favorite Ambassador.

Contents

Preface

What is an Ambassador? And what does an Ambassador mean in the context of business?

First, let's start with the history of the concept of ambassadors. Although this book is not about the neighboring countries in Europe, or the Pope, or Ferdinand of Spain, the following description taken from "Lectures On Jurisprudence" reveals an interesting comparison between the use of ambassadors in ancient Europe and the concept of Ambassadors in business today:

> When nations came to have a great deal of business one with another, it was found necessary to send messengers betwixt them, who were the first ambassadors. Anciently, as there was little commerce carried on between different nations, ambassadors were only sent on particular occasions and were what we now call ambassadors extraordinary, who returned home after their business was transacted. The first time that resident ambassadors were employed was in the beginning of the 17th century, by Ferdinand, King of Spain. Even the word ambassador comes from the Spanish verb ambassare, to send (Wicquefort, L'Ambassadeur et ses fonctions [1681], 4). The Pope indeed from the earliest times had residents, or legates, at all the courts of Europe. The very same reason that makes embassies now so frequent induced the Pope

formerly to fall upon this method. He had business in all the countries of Europe and a great part of his revenue was collected from them, and as they were continualy attempting to infringe the right he claimed, he found it necessary to have a person constantly residing at their courts to see that his priviledges were preserved. The Pope from this custom derived several advantages. When commerce was introduced into Europe, and the priviledges of every country, with the duties payable on goods in another, were settled, the merchants of one country had constant claims on those of another; they themselves were strangers in these countries, and would very readily be injured and oftener think themselves so. It became necessary therefore to have one of their countrymen constantly residing at the courts of different nations to protect the rights of his fellow subjects. Anciently, as was observed, there was little intercourse with different nations and therefore no occasion for resident ambassadors; but now, as there is something almost every day to adjust betwixt dealers, it is necessary that there should be some person of weight and authority who has access to the court, to prevent any occasion of quarrel betwixt them. We have already observed that it was Ferdinand of Spain who established this practice.

—Taken from "Lectures On Jurisprudence" [1762], edited by R. L. Meek, D. D. Raphael, and P. G. Stein, Vol. V of the *Glasgow Edition of the Works and Correspondence of Adam Smith* (Indianapolis: Liberty Fund, 1982)

Whether considering the ambassadors of ancient Europe or the Ambassadors in business today, the basic concept remains the same.

Whether an entrepreneur, business owner, or salesperson, empowering others to promote your business and to be your eyes and ears—to bring back important information to you in times when you yourself cannot be present—is an effective and powerful way to develop new business.

The Ambassador relationship is the ultimate relationship in sales. Consider the other possible relationships you may have with your customers. In the beginning of the sales process, you are a *seller*—one of many sellers competing for the business of your prospect. Then, after winning the business, you become a *supplier*—one of many suppliers who sell the same products and services you offer to your customer. Next, you become a *vendor*—one of a few vendors who sell the same products and services to your customer. Then, if you become a *partner,* you are the only one who provides your particular products and services to your customer. Finally, the *Ambassador* relationship is such that not only is your customer a *partner* but he or she is so impressed with you and the services you provide that he or she promotes you and your business to other potential customers, even without your being present.

The purpose of this book is to offer proven strategies to win Ambassadors—also known as *champions, advocates,* or *influencers*—and to empower others to promote and even sell your products and services or solutions. From developing your Ideal Ambassador Profile (IAP) and working with multiple decision makers, to working with vertical markets and channels, as well as winning Ambassadors in the press, these ideas will help you sell more in less time than you ever thought possible. I've not only included examples of how these strategies have worked in my own business, but I've also provided step-by-step guidance as to how you can apply them to your business as well. In addition,

I've offered some powerful online resources and articles to assist you in your quest for winning Ambassadors. Consider this book your Winning Ambassadors Guidebook.

At the end of each chapter, you will find a "Points to Ponder and ACTions to Take" section. This tool was designed specifically to help you put into practice the ideas and concepts presented in this book. The "Points to Ponder" section includes key points from the chapter for you to consider as they pertain to the topics at hand. The "What I Have as Shown by the Three R's" piece encourages you to consider the resources, relationships, and reciprocity available to you pertinent to the topics presented in the chapter. You will be asked to think about and write down the resources you have access to and the relationships you have that may be of help, and you will be invited to consider how you can reciprocate, or give back to, your Ambassadors in ways that are particularly relevant to the ideas presented in the chapter. By completing all the "Points to Ponder and ACTions to Take" sections at the end of each chapter, you will have a comprehensive guide and plan of ACTion to winning Ambassadors and empowering others to promote your business.

In the pages ahead, my hope is that you will embrace and put into practice the techniques described because they will enable you to truly work smarter and earn more, while at the same time enjoying the journey along the way.

Acknowledgments

Several years ago I met someone who would turn out to be not only a mentor and friend but also a true inspiration, without whom this book would not have come to be. His name is Gerhard Gschwandtner. A successful entrepreneur, author, and a leader in his field, he taught me that anything is possible, and for that I am truly grateful. Thanks, Gerhard. Every aspiring entrepreneur and author should hope for a mentor as remarkable as you.

The idea for this book was motivated by the numerous Ambassador relationships I've come to enjoy over the past several years. While I wish I could thank them all by name, in an effort to keep this short and sweet, I'll just say "thanks" and "you know who you are." It is these relationships that have inspired me to think and write about the dynamics of such connections. In addition to the genuine friendships that evolve, making these associations is a powerful way to promote and develop business to an entirely new level I never thought possible. I can only hope that the Ambassadors in my life have enjoyed the relationship as much as I have.

I'd also like to thank my family and closest friends who have always offered their support in all of my endeavors: my parents, Bill and Lola Sittig; my husband, Brian Rolf; my sisters Katy Faas and Janet Sittig; my brother Carl Sittig; and my friends Doug and Kay Bickerstaff, Heidi Hough Webster, Judy Steel, Sandy Jones-Kaminski, Lauriann Reynolds, Michael Norton, and Peter Callaghan.

Tom Kennedy, thank you for your generosity in allowing me to write about our work together so that readers can learn from real examples that illustrate the techniques described in the book. I've enjoyed our working relationship and appreciate that we have become friends in the process.

Donya Dickerson and the team at McGraw-Hill had the foresight to see the possibilities for such a book, and I am especially grateful for not only their editing expertise but also for keeping me on track and helping me stay focused throughout the process of writing this book. Donya, you have made me a better writer. Thanks!

And last, I want to especially thank those of you who will read this book. My desire for you is that it will guide you through the journey of establishing and creating sincere Ambassador relationships that will have a profound effect on your business and on your life.

POWER
REFERRALS

ACT: **A**cquire, **C**ultivate, **T**each

Don't wait. The time will never be just right.
—Napoleon Hill

How do you *win* Ambassadors? First, you have to *identify* them. Consider your prospects, customers, referral partners, networking colleagues, vendors, casual acquaintances, friends, and family. Just about everyone you know has the potential to become one of your Ambassadors; you simply must ACT: **A**cquire, **C**ultivate, and **T**each them to promote your business.

My quest for winning Ambassadors has been going on since I started my career in sales more than 17 years ago, but the Aha moment of a formal process for doing it came somewhat unexpectedly.

Two years ago I sold my company's one-day sales training program called "The Blitz Experience" to a Seattle-based office equipment and services company. I did not know at the time that this small office equipment and services company was actually part of a huge network of channel partners of a global Fortune 20 information technology corporation, which I'll call the "AB Corporation" for the purpose of confidentiality. After my initial "Blitz Pitch" to Dan, the vice president of sales at the office equipment and services company, he said he liked what he heard and wanted to move forward. He then explained to me the creative way in which he intended to pay for my sales training services.

Apparently, his company had access to channel marketing dollars from AB Corporation for sales training programs just like The Blitz Experience. In fact, AB Corporation had set money aside, money called "market development funds" but also known as "co-op funds." This term refers to dollars that are used cooperatively to benefit both AB Corporation and the manufacturer, as well as their channel partners. These market development funds are designed specifically to allow AB Corporation channel partners to participate in sales and marketing programs and initiatives that will increase the sale of AB Corporation solutions to the end user through their channel partners—such as the office equipment and services company to whom I had sold The Blitz Experience. As it turned out, The Blitz Experience was an ideal program in which to use the market development funds that were available to my newest customer.

Dan then asked if I would like him to invite his AB Corporation representative to come and observe my program. "Yes, please!" I said enthusiastically, as I realized the true opportunity that lay ahead.

The AB Corporation representative was so impressed with the impact The Blitz Experience program had on her company's sales of solutions to end users that she invited me to join a conference call that included her manager as well as her seven peers across the country. Thus, my first Ambassador was born. The rest, as they say, is history, and without even knowing it, I had begun my quest in *winning Ambassadors*.

> *Just about everyone you know has the potential to become one of your Ambassadors; you simply must ACT: Acquire, Cultivate, and Teach them to promote your business.*

Creating the **I**deal **A**mbassador **P**rofile

It is important to identify the prospects who will have the highest need for your product or service. These are your best prospects—the ones who are most likely to buy, use, and recommend you and your services.

—*Tony Alessandra*

As I mentioned in the beginning of this chapter, before you can *win* Ambassadors, you must first *identify* them. By defining the characteristics of your ideal Ambassador, you create the IAP: the **I**deal **A**mbassador **P**rofile.

The IAP consists of the traits that make up your ideal Ambassador. For example, think about what makes the person "ideal" by considering the answers to the following questions regarding each of your prospective Ambassadors:

→ What is your association with this person?
- Colleague or associate?
- Acquaintance?
- Friend?
- Family?

The association you have with a prospective Ambassador will determine where you can start in the process of developing the Ambassador relationship. In other words, the closer you

are to someone, or the better you know the person, the faster
you can realize his or her potential for being your Ambassador.
If you approach your colleagues, associates, or acquaintances
with the idea of their becoming your Ambassadors, you may
have to start with the basics of what you do and how they can
help you. It also may take a little more effort on your part to
show them how they can actually benefit from becoming your
Ambassadors. When starting from the beginning with Ambassador prospects you're not particularly close to, you will need
to focus on what's in it for them. For those with whom you
have well-established relationships, such as friends and family, the process of empowering them as Ambassadors will not
take as long because they already know you and are familiar
with what you do.

→ What company does this person represent?
   • Manufacturing company?
   • Channel dealer?
   • Channel partner?
   • Service provider?

The answer to this question will help to determine specifically
the application of your products, services, or solutions within
the context of whom this prospective Ambassador represents.
So, for example, if your Ambassador prospect represents a
manufacturing company, he or she is likely in a position to
promote your business to dealers and/or partners that are
responsible for selling that manufacturer's solutions to the end
user. If, for instance, your Ambassador prospect is a channel
dealer or partner, he or she most likely represents multiple
lines from a variety of manufacturing companies and is in a
position to promote your business to those manufacturing
companies—who can in turn promote your business to their

other channel dealers and partners. Finally, if your Ambassador prospect is a service provider, he or she is in the position of promoting your business directly to customers and prospects.

→ What is this person's role at the company he or she represents?
  • VP?
  • Sales manager?
  • Account manager?
  • Salesperson?

Defining the role of your Ambassador prospect helps you understand the decision-making ability or power that person has to promote your business. If you're working with an Ambassador prospect who is a VP as opposed to a salesperson, the level of contacts that VP has will be at a higher level than that of a salesperson. That's not to say that empowering Ambassador prospects who are salespeople is not valuable; it certainly is. A salesperson has access to not only his or her customers and prospects but also to manufacturing companies, associations, and others who may be potential customers for you. Salespeople are often the best Ambassador prospects you can find because they know how to sell and promote; that's their job, so winning them over as your Ambassadors can do wonders for your business.

→ What industry does this person's company represent?
  • High tech?
  • Government?
  • Retail?
  • Education?

Knowing the industry your Ambassador prospect represents will help you develop vertical markets of Ambassadors and allow you to become an expert in those particular fields. The industry-specific Ambassador prospects you pursue will largely depend on the nature of your business and who your best end-user prospects and customers are. For example, if education is an end-user prospect for you, then pursuing Ambassador prospects in that particular vertical market would make sense. If government is an end-user client for you, then pursuing Ambassador prospects who also work in or with government clients would be ideal, and so on.

→ Who are the contacts with whom this person has influence?
  • Customers?
  • Vendors?
  • Partners?
  • Dealers?

Understanding the contacts with whom your Ambassador prospect has influence will help guide you to knowing where and with whom your business can be promoted. If your Ambassador prospect has customers who would also be perfect customers for you, then empowering your Ambassador prospect to promote your business to those people is wise. If the Ambassador prospect works with vendors who are customers or contacts particularly suited to you, then empowering the Ambassador to promote your business to his or her vendors also makes sense. The same holds true with the partners or dealers an Ambassador prospect might have; these would be ideal people for you to know as well.

→ What recommendations does this person make to contacts to help them succeed?
  • Products?
  • Services?
  • Solutions?
  • Programs?

Ambassador prospects who are in a specific position to make recommendations to their contacts are truly ideal. Ambassador prospects because their job requires them to recommend, or even promote, the contacts they have to help make their customers successful. These types of Ambassador prospects are specifically looking for solutions and offerings they can recommend to their contacts and customers because that is the very nature of their job. These Ambassador prospects are most likely known as consultants. Determining whether or not they are in a position to promote your business depends on whom or what types of businesses they make recommendations to and what types of offerings they recommend, such as products, services, solutions, and/or programs. Consultants who work in your industry can be terrific Ambassador prospects, as they are often the most open to discussions about promoting or recommending you, since they rely on their ability to provide solid recommendations and helpful suggestions to clients.

→ How does this person work with his or her contacts?
- Does he or she gather information?
- Does he or she make recommendations?
- Does he or she make decisions on behalf of his or her contacts?
- Does he or she provide funding to allow his or her contacts to pay for his or her recommendations?

How an Ambassador prospect works with contacts gives you an idea of the type of influence he or she has. So, for example, an Ambassador prospect who actually gets paid to make recommendations would be a more qualified Ambassador prospect than someone who gathers information but does not have any particular influence with contacts. If the Ambassador prospect not only makes recommendations to his or her customers but also actually provides funding for the programs and offerings he or she recommends, that is an ideal Ambassador prospect. These types of Ambassador prospects often work for manufacturing companies that go to market through channels and provide funding to their channel partners and dealers to help increase the sale of products through the channel to the end user.

The questions I have posed here are not meant as the be-all and end-all of the questions you answer to develop your IAP. Rather, they are meant to get you thinking about what is required to fully develop your IAP. Once you've answered these questions regarding each of your Ambassador prospects, as well as more questions you develop on your own, you will have created your Ideal Ambassador Profile. In addition to finding individual potential Ambassadors based on your IAP, you may find that the IAP will also lead to certain industries or specific vertical markets and channels where you might find great Ambassador prospects as well.

> *By defining the characteristics of your ideal Ambassador, you create the IAP, the Ideal Ambassador Profile.*

Acquiring Ambassadors

Now that you've created your IAP, you are ready to ACT. Acquiring Ambassadors starts with leveraging your current relationships and converting those you already have into becoming your initial Ambassadors. Chances are you already have Ambassador relationships but don't know it, or haven't defined them as such. Acquiring Ambassadors simply requires taking these existing relationships to the next level.

The process of acquiring Ambassadors is much like that of carrying out the sales process. Think about it: Closing the sale is not as much about the *end* of the sales process as it is about the *beginning* of the sales process. And *closing* the sale is not some slick way of asking for the order but rather the *entire process* of making the sale. In other words, if you do everything right during the process of making the sale, it will just make sense to do business at the end of the day.

This holds true when acquiring Ambassadors as well. Here's an analogy: asking for the order prematurely in the sales process, a common mistake made by salespeople, is like asking someone to marry you after the first date. Too often we ask for the sale prematurely instead of giving the sales process a chance to work to our advantage by making sure we've crossed the T's and dotted the I's—that is, we've covered all our bases first.

You may have heard the expression "Don't quit five minutes before the miracle." In other words, if you're not persistent when following up with Ambassador prospects, you may make a final attempt to contact them just before they're ready to begin working with you.

Most of us are so concerned with being a "pest" that we err on the side of not being persistent enough. In my experience, it takes anywhere from 4 to 10 attempts at following up after the initial meeting to get a response from the Ambassador prospect and move to the next level in the process of working together. Many times Ambassador prospects don't get right back to us simply because they are busy. So it's important to be both patient and persistent.

There are a few things you can do to increase your likelihood of connecting with your Ambassador prospect during the follow-through:

→ First and foremost, always, always, always send a handwritten thank-you note after the first meeting, before making any follow-up phone calls or sending any e-mail. If you're able to include an article that's relevant to the prospect's business or some other item of interest to him or her, include that as well. Do not use the thank-you note as a means of selling; use it only to thank the Ambassador prospect and offer additional valuable information.

→ Call your Ambassador prospect's cell phone number rather than his or her office phone number. When calling the cell phone number, if you don't reach the Ambassador prospect but instead get voice mail, don't leave a message. Cell phones these days list the phone numbers of missed calls; and let's face it, these days businesspeople can't afford to pass up an opportunity, so it behooves them to return every call. They are curious to know who called when they miss a call from someone who didn't leave a message, so they're likely to return the call.

→ If you prefer to leave a voice mail message, tell the Ambassador prospect that you have a couple more questions to ask rather than saying you have answers to some of the questions he or she might have had.

→ If you did send an e-mail as a follow-up after the initial meeting and the Ambassador prospect hasn't responded within a week, send the exact same e-mail again one week after sending it the first time. You can keep track of the e-mails you send in Outlook either in a folder or as a "to-do" item on your calendar. Send the same initial follow-up e-mail you sent three times, one week apart. Usually by the third time you send it, you will get a response.

Also, try alternating phone calls with sending e-mails so that you give the Ambassador prospect the option of either calling you back or sending an e-mail.

There is a limit to how often to follow up and for what length of time to continue following up. If the Ambassador prospect is completely unresponsive after you've sent the same e-mail three times and have left several voice mail messages over a period of a month or more, stop for now. If the Ambassador prospect ignores you after your many attempts to communicate, this shows either a lack of interest or that something has happened in the prospect's business or personal life that is preventing him or her from getting back to you.

Before giving up completely on the follow-through, however, I recommend doing two things:

→ Wait two months between your last attempt at contact and your next attempt. Often, after some time has passed, it will be easier to reach the Ambassador prospect. Things may have settled in his or her personal or business life, if that in fact was the reason the prospect didn't get back to you initially. It could be that the person still needs your product or service but has simply forgotten about it since meeting with you.

→ As a final attempt only, you can try a technique I call the "take-away." The take-away technique leaves it up to the prospect to call you when he or she is ready to proceed. It goes something like this:

Hi Mr. Ambassador Prospect, this is Andrea Sittig-Rolf with Sittig Incorporated. I've made several attempts to contact you since our first meeting and have not been able to reach you. I understand you are very busy and that you haven't had a chance to get back to me. I won't be contacting you again, so please feel free to contact me when you're ready to proceed with the partnership we discussed. I can be reached at 206–769–4886. Thank you.

Now I know what you're thinking: it's risky. Yes, it is. That's why it's designed to be used only as a final attempt. When you've reached the point where it's obvious to you that the Ambassador prospect is no longer interested or has decided on another solution, try this technique as a last resort. You'll be surprised how often this approach will finally get a response. The theory behind this technique is that it is human nature to want to hold on to something we think is going to be taken away from us, even if we don't want the thing that's being taken away. This phenomenon starts when we're little and we lose interest in a toy until our little brother wants to play with it; then we want it back. In adolescence we see this same phenomenon when we lose interest in someone we're dating until someone else shows interest in that person; then suddenly we're interested again. The principle is the same in business. If the Ambassador prospect thinks you're going away, if there is any interest at all in working with you now or in the future, he or she will often finally respond.

Taking it to the next level, think of a time one of your contacts offered you a referral. As great as that was, wouldn't it have been even better if he or she had personally introduced you to the other person instead? Or, imagine that rather than offering you the referral or even personally introducing you, your contact actually promoted you and your business to the referral without your being present at the meeting. This is the definition of a true Ambassador—someone who promotes you and your business when you're not even there.

Other Methods of Acquiring Ambassadors

One tactic for acquiring Ambassadors is to be the best at what you do. Believe me, when you are the best, you will be noticed by your customers, prospects, vendors, and everyone else who knows you. Being an expert in your field, and being perceived as such, will give you the attention you need to acquire Ambassadors. It's important that people considering becoming Ambassadors for you are proud of their association with you. In other words, being people who know you and work with you actually makes them look good.

Also, become an invaluable resource for your contacts and it will be easy to convert them to Ambassadors. Let me explain what I mean. Several years ago while cold calling to schedule appointments to present The Blitz Experience, I spoke with a sales manager who used the fact that he was new to the job as the reason not to meet. He said, "I'm brand new to my position and I'm still getting settled, so it would probably be best if you called back in a few months." I replied, "I'd be happy to do that, but the fact that you're new to your position is the very reason we should meet now. I can be a great resource to you in your new role, and our program will make you a hero in the eyes of your superiors and your salespeople!" With that, he accepted the meeting, and as a result I did become the resource to him that I promised I would be, and that meeting led to the single largest account in my career as a sales professional. Because I followed through with my promise, he has continued to promote my products to his peers and other contacts.

The concept of being an invaluable resource can even extend beyond what you do or sell for a living. It can also mean helping someone you know get a job, helping a company you know hire the right person, donating to a charity one of your contacts cares about, and any other number of things. The point is that being genuinely focused on helping other people will reap tremendous rewards by their helping you in return. This is known as the *Rule of Reciprocity*, a fundamental and basic norm in human culture. The rule states that a person try to repay what another person has provided, and it is a part of our human nature.

There are several interesting characteristics about the Rule of Reciprocity. The first is that it is so powerful it often overwhelms the influence of what might normally determine compliance with a particular request. Second, it seems to apply to even those favors that are uninvited or unrequested. Lastly, the application of the rule can create uneven exchanges: because we humans don't like the feeling of indebtedness, we will tend to agree to a request for an even larger favor than was initially provided to us, whether the favor was requested by us or not.

Being the best at what you do, becoming an invaluable resource, and applying the Rule of Reciprocity will help you to acquire Ambassadors as you begin your quest to win Ambassadors.

Acquiring Ambassadors is just the start to winning Ambassadors, and it's the first necessary step in the overall process. On that note, keep in mind that winning Ambassadors is a *process* and not something that happens overnight; however, once your network of Ambassadors is established, it's fairly easy to maintain, and it will do wonders for growing your business with very little effort on your part in the long run.

The Rule of Reciprocity states that a person try to repay what another person has provided, and it is a part of our human nature.

Cultivating Ambassador Relationships

For every sale you miss because you're too enthusiastic, you will miss a hundred because you're not enthusiastic enough.

—Zig Ziglar

When was the last time you sent an article, press release, or news story to a client that was of particular interest to him or her that had nothing to do with what you sell? How about calling a client just to check in and say "hi" without trying to sell something? Or what about sending a client a handwritten, noncompany logo thank-you note as a token of thanks for doing business together? These are all examples of activities that will help cultivate the relationships you've created with your Ambassadors.

Years ago when I was engaged to be married, one of my vendors sent me a great article she found in the newspaper about wedding planning. She included a handwritten note congratulating me on my engagement, along with a reference to the enclosed article. Nowhere in the note did she say anything about the deal we were working on together. When it came time to make a decision about purchasing the item she was selling, all other things being equal among the other vendors I was considering, she was the one I remembered, and ultimately she was the one I gave my business to.

Here's an idea to stay on top of the subjects your Ambassadors are most interested in. Create Google Alerts. Google Alerts are e-mail updates of the latest relevant Google results (Web, news, and so on) based on your choice of query or topic. Some handy uses of Google Alerts include the following:

→ Monitoring a developing news story
→ Keeping current on a competitor

→ Getting the latest on a celebrity or event
→ Keeping tabs on your favorite sports teams
→ Generating sales leads
→ Observing financial market trends
→ Tracking prospects and customers
→ Staying up-to-date on industry news

As you get to know your Ambassadors, you'll learn what their interests are, and then you can create Google Alerts based on these topics so you'll be in-the-know at all times. They'll be impressed with how much you know about their hobbies, business interests, favorite sports teams, and other topics they care about. To find it, type www.google.com/alerts into your browser.

Staying in touch with prospects, customers, and other contacts seems an obvious way to cultivate Ambassadors, but when was the last time you proactively put a plan together for this activity and actually implemented it on a regular basis? You know what they say about planning: "Those who fail to plan, plan to fail." So make a plan and do it.

Make a list of all of your Ambassadors with their contact information. Check in once or twice a quarter. Remember, the idea with "checking in" is that there is no deal or project going on at the moment, which adds to the effectiveness and appeal of "calling for no reason." What will often happen is that during the course of the conversation, your Ambassador will mention an opportunity for you to work together, or he or she may bring up the name of someone to introduce you to who has an upcoming project that might need your help. By checking in with your Ambassador, you will allow these new opportunities to happen because you have become top-of-mind with that person. These new opportunities may remain undiscovered if you don't check in on a regular basis.

Two other ideas for checking in with potential Ambassadors are e-mail campaigns and newsletters. Often I find that after sending my monthly newsletter I get a deluge of orders on my Website for books and other products, as well as sign-ups for speaking events even though there was no mention of products in my mailing. The idea is to provide valuable information that is of interest to your Ambassadors without the motive of selling. Checking in via phone calls, e-mail campaigns, and newsletters can be highly effective for cultivating Ambassador relationships.

In our world of iPods, cell phones, and e-mail, we should not lose sight of the personal touch when it comes to maintaining contact. Handwritten notes go a long way in terms of making an impression on Ambassadors. Especially effective is sending a handwritten note on a purchased greeting card. Take the time to select a card specifically for the recipient with a picture on the front that will appeal to the person or with a message on the inside that is particularly relevant. Choosing an envelope that is a bright color and using a stamp rather than a mail meter are two other steps you can take to ensure that your note will be read. What is said in the note does not have to be lengthy or elaborate. *What* you say is actually less important than *that* you say . . . something, anything. Simply commenting on the picture on the front of the card or the message inside and writing "I saw this card and thought of you" is enough to make a good impression.

One of my customers actually sends me a handwritten thank-you note after each presentation I do with his team. I've saved every one of them, and I proudly display them in my office. Handwritten notes have such appeal because we rarely get them anymore. The fact that someone has taken the time to sit down and write something to us makes us feel special. We tend to open handwritten notes first, before any other mail that may be on our desk, and chances are we'll keep it and even post it for others to see.

By checking in, you allow new opportunities to happen.

Teaching Ambassadors to Promote your Business

The mediocre teacher tells. The good teacher explains. The superior teacher demonstrates. The great teacher inspires.
—*William Arthur Ward*

Oprah says, "You get in life what you have the courage to ask for." And she's right! Have you ever sold a car and got more than your asking price? Have you ever had a client offer to pay you more than you were asking? When negotiating to buy a house, has the seller ever offered to sell it to you for less than what you were willing to pay? Of course not! By having the courage in life to ask for what we want, we are more likely to get it than by not asking.

Like many college students living away from home for the first time, during my first year I spent more time socializing than studying. At the end of my first semester, I was mortified to learn I had a failing grade in math based on a miserable grade on the final exam. Because the rest of my grades weren't that great either, it meant I'd be on probation and would have to sit out the next semester. Given that my parents were paying for my college education and fully expected me to attend four straight years in a row, I was not excited to share the news with them.

So rather than tell my parents right away, I scheduled a meeting with my math teacher. I basically fell on my sword and apologized profusely for my embarrassing grade and asked her to let me take the final exam again, promising, of course, to study and be better prepared. To my delight and surprise, she agreed! I took the final exam again, and I did well enough to bring my final math grade up to a C, allowing me to stay the next semester and continue my college education as originally planned. Fortunately I learned this hard lesson early in my college career, which allowed me to significantly improve my GPA from then until graduation day. The point is, had I not had the courage to ask my math teacher for a second chance, I would have had to sit out a semester in college, and who knows how that would have affected my future. I asked for what I wanted, and I got it.

There is no shame in asking for help, nor is there shame is asking others to help promote your business. The beautiful thing is that Ambassadors will gladly promote you if you give them enough reason to.

One of my students, named David, took this advice to heart when calling on an existing customer where he suspected there might be additional opportunities to sell his solutions. When David asked his main contact, John, for a referral to other decision makers within the account, John gladly complied. What David did next was brilliant in that he asked John to *personally introduce* him to the contacts he had just mentioned. John also agreed to do this for David. To make a long story short, after meeting with John and the other decision makers at this particular account, David closed a $4 million dollar deal, all because he had the courage to ask for help working the account.

In addition to asking for what you want, teaching Ambassadors to promote your business also requires your becoming actively involved in their functions, networks, and spheres of influence. By doing so, you will become a part of their everyday world and you will be viewed as an insider rather than an outsider—part of the family, if you will.

Recently I was invited to attend a conference put on by one of my biggest high-tech manufacturing clients who primarily uses channel partners to go to market and sell the company's solutions to end users. As a part of the conference, the company had an evening event called the "Solutions Fair" featuring approved vendors who had products, services, and programs proven effective as strategies to increase the sales of their solutions through their channel partners.

This event allowed me to showcase my program and share how it had been used more than 60 times in the last two years to empower the company's channel partner salespeople to schedule appointments with prospects who would then sell my client's solutions to the end users. I was able to reconnect with managers who had a cluster of channel partners I had already worked with, as well as meet new managers with channel partners they had in mind for my program. Because I was actively involved in their function and I was viewed as a part of their overall organization, I was positioned for the utmost success in developing new opportunities within their company. I was introduced to a dozen new managers who each had a specific opportunity with a channel partner in mind.

Because I was *personally* introduced by one of their peers, my credibility was established immediately, and there was no "selling" involved on my part. The follow-up to this function was as simple as sending an e-mail with my upcoming availability to facilitate events for their partners. This tactic for teaching Ambassadors to promote your business works extremely well with customers that go to market using channels such as resellers, dealers, and channel partners to sell their products and services to end users. Chapter 5 will go into more detail on the topic of working with channel partners.

The final strategy in teaching Ambassadors to promote your business is creating the Ambassador Toolkit, and then rolling it out to your Ambassadors.

You get in life what you have the courage to ask for.
—Oprah Winfrey

The Ambassador Toolkit

By providing your Ambassadors with the tools they need, you make it easy for them to promote you. Ambassador Toolkits can be shared in many ways, including giving them away at events or mailing or personally delivering them to your Ambassadors.

The first step in designing your Ambassador Toolkit is to highlight the outcome you have created for others as a direct result of your solution, which you would describe in the form of a "case study."

A case study tells a short story of your customer's business challenge, the solution you've provided, the result of your solution, and a testimonial from your customer that speaks to his or her satisfaction with the result you have provided. Regardless of the features, or even the benefits, of your product or service, prospects want to know the bottom line, and that is, what results have you provided for others that you might also be able to provide for me?

Writing a case study doesn't have to be complicated, and it can actually be quite simple if you follow this basic formula—*customer name, business challenge, solution and/or result,* and *testimonial.*

For example, let's say you sell for ABC Video Conferencing Services Co., and you have provided a solution with a favorable result to your customer, XYZ Co. The case study might look something like the "Sample Case Study" that follows.

Sample Case Study

Customer: XYZ Co.

Business challenge: XYZ has executives based in multiple locations across the country who need to meet on a regular basis. Travel has become costly and time-consuming, but visual contact is an important factor in conducting their executive meetings.

Solution: ABC Video Conferencing Services provided a video-conferencing solution to allow XYZ executives to meet on a regular basis, from the comfort and convenience of each executive's own office, while still allowing the visual contact necessary for viewing of the other executives, as well as charts, graphs, and other visual aids.

Result: XYZ has reduced its travel expenses by 18 percent while still allowing executives to effectively communicate, virtually face to face.

Testimonial: "While ABC Video Conferencing Services provided excellent customer service and technical support, more important, our executives have become more efficient in their face-to-face communication, and the money we have saved on travel expenses has been applied, as profit, directly to our bottom line. Thank you, ABC Video Conferencing Services Co."—Joe Customer, president, XYZ Co.

It is important to quantify the results by referring to specifics, such as the 18 percent reduction in travel expenses shown in the Sample Case Study. You can also use a dollar amount to quantify the results you have provided. It is also very powerful if you can speak to how your solution has affected the profit of your customer.

It's a good idea for you, or someone in your company, to write the case study, rather than for your customer to write it, for a couple of reasons. First, it makes it easy for your customer to help you, because all he or she has to do is simply review and approve what you've written, rather than actually write the case study, which may not happen in the timely fashion you're hoping for. Second, by writing your own case study, you are in control of the message you want to convey, and you can speak specifically to the points you want to get across to your audience, or in this case, prospects.

You can also write the testimonial as if it were written by your customer, if it isn't already available from your customer, as long as you have permission from that customer to do so.

Your case study should be no more than 100 words and should easily fit on one 8-1/2 by 11-inch page. Case studies are also great sales tools to display on your company Website, in your marketing materials, and in your company press kits. If you have a low budget for marketing materials, case studies are ideal because you can simply print them on company letterhead where they are still very effective in creating curiosity, conveying your message, and garnering credibility.

As you can see, regardless of the size of your company or your marketing budget, you can leverage the relationships you have with your happy customers by building effective case studies. This powerful tool will help to win Ambassadors and aid in your efforts to continue to develop your Ambassador network.

In addition to case studies, your Ambassador Toolkit should include the following items:

→ A hardcopy brochure, collateral, or marketing piece designed specifically with your Ambassadors in mind. Highlight any work you've previously done with their companies by including case studies and testimonials from those who have used your solutions in the past. If you are just beginning to work with a new customer and don't have previous work with that customer to speak to, include case studies and testimonials showcasing the work you've done with others in that industry.

→ Electronic versions of the above-mentioned collateral should also be provided. Have made a leather-bound flash drive with your logo on it, and then burn any electronic information you have that is pertinent to the Ambassador's company or industry so that he or she may have the information as well as share it with others. You can also include a "live" word-processed document that has any pertinent URLs linked such that your reader can simply click on the links provided to learn even more about what you have to offer. If your company has any radio or TV coverage, include it on the flash drive too.

→ Any media coverage your company has had should also be included, such as magazine or newspaper articles and/or online articles.

→ Anything you or an executive at your company has written, such as articles, columns, and books, should also be included. These items especially help to establish credibility with your Ambassadors and show you and those at your company as experts in your field.

One final fun idea as you develop your network of Ambassadors is to have items created for them with your company logo that actually contain the word "Ambassador." So, for example, my company does quarterly mailings that include a new item that says "Ambassador, The Blitz Experience" imprinted directly on the item. Make sure the items you have created with this type of imprint are not consumable. In other words, you want them to be around so that when your Ambassador uses the item, others will see it and ask about it. Make sure the items are of high quality. A couple of items to consider are leather-bound portfolios (that is, notepad holders), pens, or any other item your Ambassador would use for business while out and about with customers and contacts.

Once you've put your Ambassador Toolkit together, you are ready to use it as an effective tool to teach your Ambassadors how to promote you and your business.

By providing your Ambassadors with the tools they need, you make it easy for them to promote you.

FREE TOOLS

Go to www.sittiginc.com, click on the *Power Referrals* icon, and download the "Ideal Ambassador Profile Template," the "Case Studies Templates," the "Ambassador Toolkit Checklist," and the "ACTions to Take Worksheet."

Points to Ponder and ACTions to Take

Points to Ponder

- How do you *win* Ambassadors? First, you have to *identify* them.
- The IAP consists of the traits that make up your ideal Ambassador.
- Acquiring Ambassadors starts with leveraging your current relationships and converting those you already know into becoming your initial Ambassadors.
- Create Google Alerts to stay informed about news your Ambassadors care about.
- New opportunities may remain undiscovered if you don't check in with your Ambassadors on a regular basis.
- There is no shame in asking for help, nor is there shame is asking others to help promote your business.
- The first step in designing your Ambassador Toolkit is to highlight the outcome you have created for others as a direct result of your solution, which you describe in the form of a "case study."
- Once you've put your Ambassador Toolkit together, you are ready to use it as an effective tool to teach your Ambassadors how to promote you and your business.

What I Have as Shown by the Three R's

Resources

Relationships

Reciprocity (How can I give back to my Ambassadors as it relates to this topic?)

What I Need

How I Will Get What I Need

ACTion Step 1

ACTion Step 2

ACTion Step 3

ACTion Step 4

ACTion Step 5

2

Mindset

Sooner or later, those who win are those who think they can.
—Richard Bach, author of the best-seller Jonathan Livingston Seagull

So much of successfully empowering Ambassadors to promote your business depends on four things—choosing a positive attitude, getting fired up, using creative visualization, and inspiring confidence. In this chapter, we'll explore the most effective ways to choose the right attitude for winning Ambassadors.

Choosing a Positive Attitude

Confidence and enthusiasm are the greatest sales producers in any kind of economy.
—O. B. Smith

You may notice I've used the phrase "*Choosing* a Positive Attitude" rather than "*Having* a Positive Attitude." I've done this purposefully to show that attitude is a choice and not something we simply "have." We decide what attitude to hold at any given time, based on a decision we made in advance of unforeseen circumstances, to positively view all that happens to us. Charles Swindoll, the evangelical Christian pastor, author, educator, and radio preacher who founded Insight for Living, sums it up nicely: "I am convinced that life is 10 percent what happens to me and 90 percent how I react to it." In many ways, we cannot control what happens to us in life, but we are 100 percent responsible for controlling how we react to what happens. Choosing to have a positive attitude is crucial to the success of empowering Ambassadors. It starts with a confident and eager mindset such that it is contagious and rubs off on other people.

Attitude is a key element for anyone who has chosen sales as a career, and let's face it, we are all salespeople to some degree, whether we're business owners or senior managers. If you are a sales professional, you know that having a positive attitude makes a world of difference in your success. In a profession that is conducive to rejection, you must have a positive attitude to be able to deal with the sometimes negative circumstances that occur simply as a result of being a salesperson.

How many times have you lost a sale and then immediately began thinking about what you could have done differently to win the business? The telling factor in your long-term success as a sales professional is your ability to learn from each "lost deal" and correct those mistakes the next time, which is all part of choosing a positive attitude.

It's amazing how far a positive attitude can take you in the world of sales. Attitude is a huge part of what makes up your reputation, and it often is one of the first things people will notice when meeting you for the first time. It's easy to have a positive attitude when things are going well; the difficulty comes in remaining positive when things don't go the way you'd hoped.

Because attitude is a mindset that reveals itself in behaviors, acting in a positive manner even when you don't feel positive will change the way you feel over time, which means you can change your attitude if you so desire.

To put a positive spin on the sometimes negative or losing circumstances that occur in sales, just think to yourself, "Yeah, losing stinks, but if it didn't happen every once in a while, I wouldn't appreciate winning!" Or, as Jimmy Dean once said, "I can't change the direction of the wind, but I can adjust my sails to always reach my destination." Replace "sails" with "sales" and you'll get the point.

Many years ago I worked for a woman who I'll call Jane out of respect for her privacy. Jane came from a broken home. She had a mother and sister. Jane's mother had to work three jobs just to stay afloat and keep her two daughters fed. Jane had excellent grades in high school, and as a result, she won a college scholarship. She went on to become a very successful businesswoman who was then able to buy her mother a beautiful home and support her for the rest of her life.

Jane's sister, on the other hand, came from the same environment as Jane but chose a different route. She didn't make good grades in school and when fairly young became pregnant with her first child. She had more children from different men over the years, and she became a drug addict. The differences between these two women were vast. One chose to work hard work, and the other turned to drugs. In all fairness to the sister, there may have been other factors, such as mental illness, that played a role in her decisions, but I was especially impressed with what Jane was able to do with her life by choosing wisely.

Her attitude was amazing. She was one of the most bubbly, animated, high-energy people I had ever met. It was obvious to me that her attitude impacted her life significantly was responsible for her success.

> **We decide what attitude to hold at any given time, based on a decision we made in advance of unforeseen circumstances, to positively view all that happens to us.**

Getting Fired Up

Success in the long run has less to do with finding the best idea, organizational structure, or business model for an enterprise, than with discovering what matters to us as individuals.

—*Jerry Porras*

Several years ago I enjoyed my first experience flying first class on a business trip to California with John, who was my boss. We were going to pitch an idea we had for developing new business to the senior management team of our prospective client. At the time, our idea was considered somewhat unusual, and a bit controversial, for our particular line of business. During the flight, John asked me to explain my thoughts on presenting our idea. I was pretty fired up about what we were doing so I enthusiastically shared my plan. (Keep in mind that John was in the window seat, and I was in the aisle seat, with my back turned from the aisle, facing John.) When I was finished, John put his hand up in the air, with the palm of his hand facing me. I naturally assumed he was congratulating me on a well-articulated plan so I yelled "High five!" and put my hand up in the air to slap his. Imagine my embarrassment when he looked at me as if I were crazy and said, "Andrea, what are you doing? I'm just trying to get some water from the flight attendant!" I slowly turned around to see the flight attendant standing in the aisle, attempting to hand John a bottle of water.

The point is that I was thrilled about what I was doing, and it was obvious. As silly as I looked to my boss, we had a good laugh and the "high five" became an ongoing inside joke between the two of us any time we had a conversation about a new plan or idea. He liked the fact that I was fired up, and so did I. If you're not fired up about what you do or what you sell, no one else will be either. If you are fired up, others will be too!

One way I encourage salespeople to get over their initial reluctance to cold calling is to tell them, "Pretend you're calling to tell someone he or she has won the lottery. Then would you feel like you were intruding or interrupting someone's day? Of course not! Remember that what you have to offer is *valuable* to your prospects and customers. It's the prospects' lucky day that you are calling because now they will have the chance to meet with you, learn about what you have to offer, and potentially solve a problem or make their life easier based on the solution that you provide." Without this mindset, it becomes very difficult to even pick up the phone, but with it, salespeople become eager to get started. They realize they're going to get out of the training what they put into it and that their attitude for the day will greatly affect their success on the phone.

> *If you're not fired up about what you do or what you sell, no one else will be either. If you are fired up, others will be too!*

Using Creative Visualization

Vision is not enough; it must be combined with venture. It is not enough to stare up the steps; we must step up the stairs.
    —*Vaclav Havel*

According to Remez Sasson (www.SuccessConsciousness.com) in an article entitled "From Imagination to Reality: Attracting Success with Mind Power," "Creative visualization is the ability to use the imagination, see images in our minds and make them come true. If we add concentration and feelings, it becomes a great creative power that makes things happen. Used in the right way, visualization can bring changes into our lives. The thought is the matrix or blueprint; the feelings provide the energy, the 'electricity.'"

Does that sound weird? It isn't at all!

This is the power of creative visualization. This is the power that can alter our environment and circumstances; cause events to happen; attract money, possessions, work, and love; change habits; and improve our health. It is a great mind power. It is the power behind every success.

By visualizing an event, a situation, or an object, such as a car, a house, or furniture, we attract it to us. We see in our imagination what we want and it happens. It is like daydreaming. It resembles magic, though actually there is no magic here. It is the natural process of the power of the thoughts.

How does it work and why? Thought is a power, and it has an effect on the material world. Thoughts, if powerful enough, travel from one mind to another. If we keep thinking the same thought, people in our environment perceive it and act on it, furthering, usually in an unconscious manner, the materialization of our desires.

Some years ago I read about a study done on the powerful concept of creative visualization. The idea behind the study was that by simply visualizing the "what," the subconscious will determine the "how." In other words, by determining what you want and focusing on it mentally by picturing your life once you have it, your subconscious will take over to figure out how to get it.

The study I read about took players on a basketball team and divided them into two groups. The first would actually practice free throwing, while the other would only visualize free throwing. Each group was given the same amount of time for the exercise. Next, each group was asked to make free throws. The number of successful free throws was exactly the same for both groups, showing the power of visualization.

Simply by visualizing, you create pathways in your brain that establish the mental piece of doing whatever it is you decide you want. Maybe this is where the saying "You can do anything you set your mind to" comes from. You're setting your mind to allow your physical body to perform in a way you desire. The beauty is you don't even have to visualize all that often or for any extended length of time. Once or twice a day for a few minutes at a time is enough to get the pathways of your brain and subconscious stimulated for ongoing visualization, even when you're not consciously aware of it.

Obviously visualization alone isn't enough to make things happen; it also requires hard work. The point is that it starts with visualizing what you want before you can begin to act on it.

You can do anything you set your mind to.

Establishing Credibility and Inspiring Confidence

Prophecy: The art and practice of selling one's credibility for future delivery.

—Ambrose Bierce

You must establish credibility with your Ambassadors to be considered an expert in your field; then, and only then, should you even think about trying to win Ambassadors. This took me 15 years to learn, and in just 15 words, I've shared with you one of the most valuable lessons of building a team of Ambassadors.

So, how do you do that? You write, speak, and help others.

Write articles, columns, newsletters, books—whatever you can write, write. Do some research on newspapers and trade magazines that don't currently cover your particular area of expertise, and approach the editor with your idea to provide an article or a column. With Internet blogs and other types of online media, you'd be surprised by how much space is actually available in newspapers and magazines that could be filled with your ideas. Many editors are open to new ideas, and they are often looking for something fresh to add to their publications.

And, while your company may provide a newsletter to its customers, there is no reason why you can't provide your own newsletter to your Ambassadors. Keep in mind that newsletters should provide value-added content and not be a way in which you blatantly advertise your products and services.

The long-term effect of writing good newsletters is that Ambassadors remember you and consider you an expert. They will therefore contact you when they have a need or know someone who has a need. Newsletters can be one of the best forms of subtle advertising if they're done right. I will go into more detail about writing newsletters in Chapter 7.

Write a book. Have you ever thought about writing a book? It probably sounds daunting, but when you truly are an expert in your field and have at least 10 years of experience in the same industry, you could easily fill the pages of a great book with your ideas and strategies. Before you begin, buy the book *The Shortest Distance Between You and a Published Book: 20 Steps to Success* (Broadway Books, 1997). In it, author Susan Page details 20 steps from idea to publication and outlines realistic time frames to help you with the process of getting a book published. In addition, purchase the book *Writer's Market*, edited by Robert Brewer. It is updated each year, so buy the most recent edition. This book will become an invaluable resource to you as you search for agents and publishers. It clearly spells out what types of books agents are looking to represent and what types of books publishers are looking to publish.

Your book is an excellent tool to include in your Ambassador Toolkit. Being a published author not only establishes credibility with the general audience you're selling to, but it also gives your Ambassadors a tool, something tangible, they can share with your prospective customers. It's one thing for your Ambassadors to talk about you and promote you verbally; it's quite another for them to share your book with their contacts, who are also your prospects, because it is a physical item that in one package represents your expertise.

As a published author, you are viewed as not just a salesperson or business owner but as a true expert in your field with skills and knowledge that will help others. You will be perceived as an authority as it relates to your specialty. An added bonus to becoming a published author is that you can easily justify increasing your rates. Prospects are willing to pay more for someone who has a proven track record, and publishing a book is one way of sharing your experience with your Ambassadors and prospects. Once you become published, it's as if you've been screened, so to speak, by an authority of sorts—that is, the publisher. In other words, a legitimate publisher is going to publish a book only if it feels the book has something important to say as it relates to the subject matter. While self-publishing is certainly an option, publication by an established, legitimate publisher provides you with a greater amount of credibility than self-publishing because, as I mentioned above, the publisher acts as a screening agent. By publishing your book, it has put its stamp of approval not only on what you have to say but on you as the person saying it.

Speaking and writing go hand-in-hand. In other words, what you write about, you can speak about. Make a list of the topics you've written about and consider them as springboards for speeches to offer to audiences in your industry or related industries. Contact your local chamber of commerce, industry associations, and other appropriate groups and offer your speaking expertise. Keep in mind that there are different kinds of speeches, including keynote, workshop, and training.

A keynote speech is generally 45 minutes to an hour in length, and it is specifically designed to address the why of a given situation, whereas a workshop is usually intended to address the how. Oftentimes chambers of commerce and other industry associations are actively looking for speakers to provide a keynote or workshop at their monthly meetings. Simply research your local chamber of commerce and industry associations online, and look for a listing of the staff, specifically the event coordinator or program coordinator. You may also find information for how to apply to become a speaker. Then, once you've been invited to speak at a public event, invite as many direct prospects and Ambassador prospects as you can to see you in action. This will give your audience the opportunity to not only become familiar with your content but also to see your presentation style.

If this information is not available online, call the main number and ask for the event or program coordinator, who will most likely be your point of contact for offering your speaking services. In addition, as you become known as a writer in your field, you may actually be contacted directly by your local chamber of commerce and industry associations and asked to speak at their upcoming events.

Unlike most keynote speeches and workshops, a training program will usually require a deeper look at your particular area of expertise, and it may require a full day or more for you to actually teach others about your specialty. Offering free training to Ambassadors to educate them about your industry, products, and services is an excellent way to establish credibility and become the "go-to" person when they have a need for your expertise or know someone who does.

Educating Ambassadors is a natural part of the winning Ambassadors process. Offering free training in a group setting—that is, with several Ambassadors at a time—allows you to train many people at once. A group setting also allows your Ambassadors to learn more about what you have to offer without the pressure of a one-on-one sales call.

Finally, helping others is an incredibly effective way to establish, or enhance, your credibility. Make an effort to learn about what your colleagues, associates, networking partners, prospects, customers, and Ambassadors want, and do what you can to help them get it.

Offer qualified leads and referrals to your Ambassadors. Help your Ambassadors get more of what they want, even if it doesn't involve selling them your products and services. Giving and offering help to others without the expectation of reciprocation often comes back tenfold, and in the process, it not only enhances your credibility but also solidifies your good reputation.

You must establish credibility with your Ambassadors to be considered an expert in your field.

Nelson Mandela said in his 1994 inaugural speech, "Our deepest fear is not that we are inadequate. Our deepest fear is that we are powerful beyond measure. It is our light, not our darkness, that frightens us most. We ask ourselves, 'Who am I to be brilliant, gorgeous, talented, and famous?' Actually, who are you not to be? . . . And when we let our own light shine, we unconsciously give other people permission to do the same. As we are liberated from our own fear, our presence automatically liberates others."

In order to inspire confidence in others and to make them comfortable with our ability to do what we promise, we must first exhibit confidence ourselves.

Several months ago while conducting a training program, I had the opportunity to listen in on a participant as she made her calls. I was impressed with the fact that she was scheduling so many appointments and that she was rarely told "no" by the prospect. When I was questioning her about what it was specifically that she was doing, outside of the techniques I had taught during my program, it became obvious that it was her tone, enthusiasm, and confidence that had so much to do with her success at securing appointments.

It's difficult to teach confidence. Most people either have it or they don't, but there is something to the saying, "Fake it until you make it." In other words, act *as if.* If you're not a confident person, pretend that you are. Eventually, your behavior will change the way you feel, and you will begin to not just *act* confidently but actually *feel confident* as well. Confidence is an attractive trait in anyone, and inspiring confidence in your Ambassadors will encourage them to promote you.

Who am I to be brilliant, gorgeous, talented, and famous? Actually, who are you not to be?

—*Nelson Mandela*

FREE TOOLS

Go to www.sittiginc.com, click on the *Power Referrals* icon, and download the "Attitude Check Worksheet," the "Inspiring Confidence Checklist," and the "ACTions to Take Worksheet."

Points to Ponder and ACTions to Take

Points to Ponder

- Attitude is a key element for anyone who has chosen sales as a career, and let's face it, we are all salespeople to some degree, whether we are business owners or senior managers.
- Attitude is a huge part of what makes up your reputation, and often it is one of the first things people will notice when meeting you for the first time.
- Remember that what you have to offer is *valuable* to your prospects and customers.
- You must establish credibility with your Ambassadors to be considered an expert in your field; then, and only then, should you even think about trying to win Ambassadors.

What I Have as Shown by the Three R's

Resources

Relationships

Reciprocity (How can I give back to my Ambassadors as it relates to this topic?)

What I Need

How I Will Get What I Need

ACTion Step 1

ACTion Step 2

ACTion Step 3

ACTion Step 4

ACTion Step 5

3

Developing Ambassadors at Your Accounts

Before you invest the time and energy going out to meet with every prospect, make certain you're meeting with the right prospect. Uncover who the decision makers are by using the following question. "By the way, is there anyone else you can think of who would be part of this evaluation and decision-making process and should therefore be included in this meeting?"

—Keith Rosen

Ideal Client Profile

The first step to learn before developing accounts and working with multiple decision makers is how to create your Ideal Client Profile (ICP). You must first understand who your targeted ideal clients and prospects are before you can devise a methodology in which to work with multiple decision makers and further develop accounts.

How many times have you actually thought about who your ideal clients are? Think about it. Think about how your business would change if it were made up of "ideal clients" because you approached the activity of prospecting with the intention of pursuing only those prospects who fit a certain profile. Consider the ideal clients you currently work with:

→ What makes them ideal?
→ What are the parameters of, or formula for, your ideal clients?
→ What size company are they?
→ How many employees do they have?
→ How much do they earn in revenue each year?
→ Who are their clients?
→ What is their product or service?
→ How many locations do they have?
→ How do they go to market (that is, direct versus indirect sales, retail, channel sales, and so on)?
→ How much revenue do you earn each year with your ideal clients?
→ Do you have repeat business with your ideal clients?
→ How many decision makers must you deal with to get a "yes" in working with your ideal clients?
→ How much client service is involved in working with your ideal clients?
→ Do your ideal clients give you referrals to other ideal clients?

Yes, these are a lot of questions to think about. But in clearly defining your ICP, it's important to think through what industries or specific vertical markets will make excellent prospects for you based on the nature of their industries or businesses. (We'll talk more about vertical markets in the next chapter.)

In defining your ICP, you can begin to focus on only those clients who fit your profile and therefore those who are the best for your business. This also allows you to quickly identify those who are *not* ideal clients and move on to those who are. Think about how much more effective you could be in attracting ideal clients when you're no longer wasting time with prospects who aren't the best fit for what you sell.

When I started my company, I initially focused on any prospect, no matter what size, that had a sales team of at least three people. Without knowing it, that is how I was defining my ICP: prospects that had a sales team of at least three people. That's it—I didn't take any other factors into consideration. This approach forced me to "start over" not only each month but literally each day to determine where my next paycheck was coming from since there was often no potential for any future business with that prospect. And believe me, that's no way to live!

I was successful at finding clients, but I was running myself ragged because they were mostly small, one-opportunity clients. It wasn't until I took the time to define my ICP that I was able to take my business to the next level and create the kind of momentum that has allowed me to quadruple my revenue since starting the company in 2002.

Now, instead of simply trying to find any business that has at least three salespeople as a prospect, I'm focused on businesses that emulate the characteristics of my ideal clients. For example, companies that go to market through channel partners and have a budget set aside specifically for marketing and/or sales training programs are ideal prospects for me. Also, manufacturing companies seem to fit the bill because they often have large sales teams. Annual revenue is another component I take into consideration when deciding whether or not to pursue a prospect. Generally, companies that do $100 million or more in sales annually are ideal prospects for my program. Once I became clear as to my true ICP, I was more focused and better organized, and my business began to take off.

In defining your Ideal Client Profile, you can begin to focus on only those clients who fit your profile.

Account Mapping

Once you identify who your ICP is, the next step is Account Mapping as shown here:

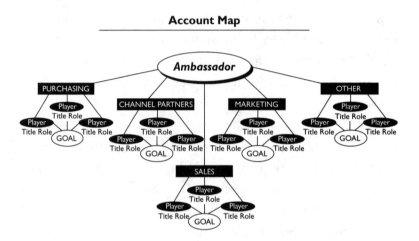

Similar to an organizational chart or flowchart, an Account Map allows you to name the key players within an account. By creating a map that describes each of their roles and responsibilities and where they stand in the corporate hierarchy, as well as their spheres of influence within the account, you can identify and empower Ambassadors within existing accounts so that you can work wider and deeper to gain even more traction.

This step is different from Account Profiling, which I will describe in the next section, in that Account Mapping is the first piece of the overall strategy in fully understanding the key players and their roles so you may then profile and penetrate the account.

Especially when working with large organizations, it is critical to understand the role of each of the key players as well as their process for working with vendors, customers, colleagues, and other business associates. Creating the Account Map allows you to focus on those key players who are most likely to become your Ambassadors.

Several resources are available online to aid in the development of creating Account Maps, including Hoover's and First Research. Hoover's offers information about industries, companies, and key decision makers for sales, marketing, business development, and other professionals who need intelligence on U.S. and global companies, industries, and the people who lead them. Find them online at www.hoovers.com.

First Research was founded in 1998 by a sales professional in the financial industry who recognized a direct correlation between the amount of time he spent preparing for and learning about a client's business and industry conditions and the success of the sales call. Today, First Research is a leading industry intelligence company that helps sales teams perform faster and smarter, open doors, and close more deals. First Research performs the "heavy lifting" by synthesizing hundreds of sources into an easy-to-digest format that a salesperson can consume very quickly to better understand a prospect's or client's business issues. First Research can be found online at www.firstresearch.com.

To further develop an Account Map at any given account, start with your best contact first—that is, the key decision maker you normally work with—and then begin defining the key players and their roles and responsibilities to gain a better understanding of the inner workings of the account. Here are some great questions you can ask your main contact that will help you define the Account Map. (Some of the answers to these questions you may already know, in which case you can simply ask your main contact to confirm the information you already have.)

→ What is the process used to make purchasing decisions?
- Who is involved in purchasing decisions?
- What are their specific roles in the purchasing process?
- Does your company sign vendor contracts, or do the vendors sign your contracts?
- What is it you are trying to accomplish with this process? What is the desired end result?

→ What is the process of working with channel partners, if any?
- Who is involved with this process?
- What are their specific roles in the process?
- Who is responsible for bringing on new channel partners?
- What is it you are trying to accomplish with this process? What is the desired end result?

→ What is your new business development or sales process?
- Who is involved with this process, and what are their specific roles?
- What is the strategy for bringing on new accounts?
- What is the strategy in working with existing accounts?
- What is it you are trying to accomplish with this process? What is the desired end result?

→ What is your marketing process?
- Who is involved with this process?
- What are their specific roles in the process?
- Who is responsible for leading your marketing campaigns?
- What is it you are trying to accomplish with this process? What is the desired end result?

By duplicating this line of questioning within the various departments or divisions of each account and with each of your contacts, you will create your Account Map. While it may seem like a barrage of questions, just explain to your main contact that the better you understand the account, the more helpful you can be in developing the best solution to fit the company's needs. Also remember not to ask questions you already know the answers to, or, if you do ask questions, do so in such a way that shows you are familiar with the account and just need further clarification regarding specific information you're gathering so that you can offer the best possible recommendation. In addition to the specifics you will learn as a result of asking these open-ended questions, you will also get a sense of the culture and sometimes a sense of the political landscape of the account as well. It will become obvious to you after gathering all of this information who your best Ambassador prospects are, and you can begin to focus on those individuals as you ACT.

Creating the Account Map allows you to focus on those key players who are most likely to become your Ambassadors.

Account Profiling

Different from Account Mapping, Account Profiling involves determining the set of characteristics or qualities of an account that help to identify it as a specific type of company. As you go through the exercise of profiling accounts, you will begin to see a pattern of the types of accounts where you are most likely to win Ambassadors.

Some of the crucial information you must gather to develop each Account Profile includes but is not limited to the following:

→ Corporate structure (see Account Map)
→ Public relations
→ News stories and/or press releases

→ Financial documents or annual reports (if available)
  • Stock value (if it is a publicly held company)
→ Industry
  • Trends
  • Events and/or trade shows
  • Media (magazines, radio, TV, and so on)
→ Key initiatives
→ Business performance issues
→ Competitive information

Gathering this type of information is valuable in that it forces you to truly understand what you know and don't know about each account. It will be obvious what gaps there are in your knowledge of each account, which then allows you to determine the additional information you still require for a complete Account Profile. Once you have analyzed the data you have collected, you should be able to form an opinion about how you could work with this account. Once you have amassed the information and can offer your perspective of what it means, you can ACT.

Developing an Account Profile for each of your account's competitors will also give you a plethora of information about the competitive environment as well as a profile of other potential Ambassadors. Any time you create an effective Ambassador relationship within one account, that account's competitors become prospects for you as well, given the fact that you have already determined a fit for what you do in that particular industry. Of course, you walk a fine line here as you don't want to appear disloyal to your existing Ambassadors by working with their competitors; however, as long as you don't share confidential competitive information between accounts, you should be fine.

As you go through the exercise of profiling accounts, you will begin to see a pattern of the types of accounts where you are most likely to win Ambassadors.

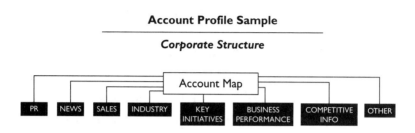

Account Profile Sample

Corporate Structure

Account Penetration

Inside the company, you'll want to achieve total account penetration. You can do this with the same person you've been working with (the original buyer) or with a different person (from another department, location, division, branch, subsidiary, or sister company).

—*Tony Alessandra*

Ever get the feeling the receptionist has been trained just to screen your calls and keep you from connecting with your Ambassador prospect? Well, guess what, she has! The first step in penetrating accounts is getting through that initial barrier, often called the "Gatekeeper," so that you can connect with your Ambassador prospect and begin the process of working together. Luckily, there are a few tricks you can use to do just that.

First, engage the receptionist. Then, be genuine in your approach. Receptionists can smell a rat from hundreds of miles away; that's part of their training too.

Many times, just by logging on to a company Website, you can find the name of the CEO or president of the company. Make a note of this information before you place your call. Let's say the CEO of the company you're calling on is John Jones. Now, let's take a look at how the conversation with the receptionist should go:

Receptionist: ABC Company, how can I direct your call?

Salesperson: Hi, my name is Andrea Sittig-Rolf, and I'm with Sittig Incorporated. I'm hoping you can help me. I'm looking for the person in your organization who would make a decision regarding sales training for your channel partners. That wouldn't be John Jones, would it?

Receptionist: Oh no, that wouldn't be John Jones. That would be Bob Smith.

Salesperson: Great! Can I speak to Bob, please?

Receptionist: Sure, I'll transfer you.

Salesperson: Thank you.

Believe it or not, most of the time, this technique works, and it will get you to the person you need to talk to. The idea is that the receptionist doesn't want to bother John Jones, the CEO, with a cold call from a salesperson. It's almost a relief for her to be able to transfer you to Bob Smith, someone below John Jones on the organizational chart at the company.

Even if you are unable to speak to Bob Smith during this particular phone call, at least now you have the name of the person you need to talk to for the next time you call. Receptionists don't screen calls as often when the callers have the name of the person they want to talk to.

On another note, it seems obvious but, for goodness sake, say "please" and "thank you." You would not believe the number of salespeople who don't say these words when they are dealing with receptionists, or with anyone else for that matter. Simple courtesy goes a long way.

Another tip is to ask for the sales department when the receptionist answers. Believe me, callers are not screened when calling on the sales department, for obvious reasons. Then, when you get a salesperson on the phone, say something like, "Hi. I'm not sure if you can help me, but I'm actually hoping to talk to ___ [you fill in the blank with the title of your Ambassador prospect or description of his or her role at the company]. Who would that be?" Salespeople are not trained to screen calls, and we love to talk, so chances are you'll get plenty of information about the company you're calling on as well as the person you ultimately need to talk to.

Years ago I worked with a man named Mike who had worked in the mortgage industry for many years. He knew one prospect who needed his mortgage services, but he could never get the guy to take his calls, much less schedule a meeting with him. Mike knew that this particular prospect owned a lot of commercial property and was planning to purchase more, so it behooved Mike to think of some way of getting in the door. Mike's usual methods proved unsuccessful, so he decided to use a more creative tactic. What he did next was ingenious. Mike called the prospect's assistant and asked her what the prospect's favorite shoe brand was and what size shoe he wore. Mike purchased a pair of shoes based on the description the assistant gave him, and he mailed just *one* shoe to the prospect with a note that read, "Just trying to get my foot in the door. I'll bring the other shoe to a meeting we schedule at your convenience. Give me a call." Mike enclosed his business card in the package as well.

Within minutes of receiving the shoe, the prospect called Mike to schedule a meeting. From then on, the prospect became one of Mike's best customers! Obviously this isn't a tactic you could use with all of your Ambassador prospects, but it's not a bad idea for that one you know has a need for what you do and that could lead to a mutually beneficial business relationship.

There are a lot of ways you could do something similar with your prospects. Think of anything that requires a pair to be functional, such as shoes, earrings, gloves, or even tickets to an event, and then send just one of the items to your Ambassador prospect with the promise of bringing the other one in person when you meet. We work in a competitive environment. Your potential Ambassadors have the opportunity to work with any number of your peers and competitors, so setting yourself apart is vital right from the beginning of these relationships.

Guiding Your Ambassadors

Once you connect with your Ambassador prospects, the next natural step is establishing a process of working as a team so that doing business together is seamless. Here are a couple of ideas for building your relationships with your Ambassadors.

A philosophy I live by in my business is that "the purpose of a meeting is to get another meeting." In other words, because winning Ambassadors is a *process,* the purpose of a meeting is not necessarily to win them immediately.

In most cases, you will need more than one meeting, as well as other forms of communication, such as phone conversations, e-mail exchanges, and other written correspondence, before you actually begin working with a new Ambassador. When you end your first meeting with a potential Ambassador, make it your goal to get him or her to agree to the next step. By doing this, you are ensuring that the Ambassador is willing to move through the process with you.

Also, at the end of the first meeting, after the prospective Ambassador has agreed to work with you, ask for a commitment that he or she will, in fact, respond to you when you follow up. How many times have prospects asked you to follow up, and when you do, they don't respond to you? Maddening, isn't it? If the answer to doing business together is "no," wouldn't you rather know sooner rather than later so you don't waste time trying to contact someone who isn't really an Ambassador prospect anyway.

One way to ensure that your Ambassador prospects will respond to you when you follow up is to give them an "out" if they decide not to do business with you. After you've agreed to the next follow-up step, say something like, "Can I ask you a favor? When I follow up with you in two weeks, if for some reason you've decided not to proceed, will you please let me know? There's a saying in sales that 'a fast no is better than a slow no,' and if you've decided to go another way, that's okay, just let me know so I won't waste your time or mine."

Sounds a little bold, but most Ambassador prospects will respond positively to this because it not only gives them the out they need if they decide to go another direction but it also shows them that you are a busy professional and you don't want to waste anyone's time. This technique also works well because suddenly you're not a desperate salesperson but rather a confident consultant who has something of value to offer.

Another way to persuade your Ambassadors to continue to work with you is by proving that your solution does not just show a return on investment (ROI) but actually creates a profit center for them and their companies.

For example, if by implementing the solution you provide your Ambassadors or their contacts, they will be investing $10,000 but actually saving $15,000 in other operating costs within six months, you can show not just an ROI within six months but also an actual profit (or savings) of $5,000. (Savings can also be viewed as profit since it ultimately affects the bottom line, which is probably the thing your Ambassador prospects care about most.)

Another way to get Ambassador prospects to respond to you is to be creative in how you tie your solution to your approach. Let me explain what I mean. Seventeen years ago, for my first job out of college, I worked for a company that sold voice mail services—meaning that clients would pay a monthly fee to "lease" voice mail for their offices. This arrangement was similar to what many of us do now in our homes through the local phone company rather than purchasing our own costly voice mail hardware. At the time the voice mail technology was so new that the common objection I'd get when calling receptionists to set appointments was, "What's voice mail?" and then after explaining it, I would hear, "Oh, we don't need that. We use pink slips!"

After one of my colleagues, Brad, was tired of running into this objection repeatedly, he decided it was time to *show* his prospect why using voice mail was better than using pink slips. During one of his prospecting calls, when asked by the receptionist if she could take a message for him, Brad said, "sure" and he went on to leave a lengthy message for the prospect. He then proceeded to write down his message on a pink slip, word for word, as a back-up for what he was about to do next. Brad was persistent, and he continued to call the prospect until he reached him, since the messages he was leaving were not being returned. When Brad finally met with the prospect face-to-face, he said, "Did you get the message I left the other day?" The prospect said, "Oh yeah, it's here somewhere." Then, after searching around the top of his cluttered desk, he found the pink slip on which the receptionist had written Brad's message and said, "Here it is." The prospect held up the pink slip for Brad to see, but all that was written was "Brad Smith called" and his phone number.

Nothing else was written on the pink slip, and certainly not the lengthy message Brad had actually asked the receptionist to take. Brad then showed his *own* pink slip to the prospect, on which he had written the *actual* message he left, and he said, "This is actually the message I left for you that day." The prospect, after realizing by seeing for himself the important information he was missing by not having our voice mail service, said to Brad, "Where do I sign?" And Brad walked out with a substantial order for our voice mail services! By being creative in his approach and using the lack of our voice mail technology at the prospect's office to show why voice mail was better than pink slips, Brad got the order.

Finally, creating a sense of urgency will help move the process along quickly. Doing this requires that your solution be so compelling that it doesn't make sense for your Ambassador to go another day without it. A sense of urgency is created by first emphasizing the pain your Ambassador prospect is experiencing by not having your solution and then demonstrating how your solution will help alleviate that pain.

Now all you have to do is show that the sooner your solution is implemented, the sooner the pain will go away. And from that point, it will be clear that the next logical step in the process will be to identify a project and begin working together!

Account Penetration: The purpose of a meeting is to get another meeting.

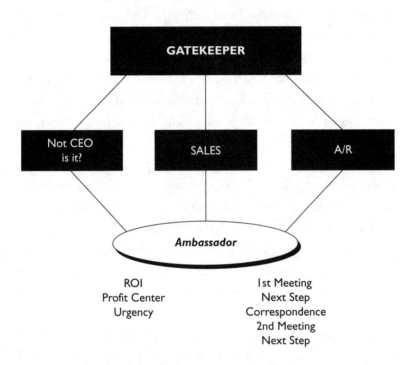

Account Penetration

ROI
Profit Center
Urgency

1st Meeting
Next Step
Correspondence
2nd Meeting
Next Step

FREE TOOLS

Go to www.sittiginc.com, click on the *Power Referrals* icon, and download the "Ideal Client Profile Template," the "Account Map Template," the "Account Profile Template," the "Account Penetration Plan of Action Worksheet," and the "ACTions to Take Worksheet."

Points to Ponder and ACTions to Take

Points to Ponder

- You must first understand who your targeted ideal clients and prospects are before you can devise a methodology in which to work with multiple decision makers and further develop accounts.
- Account Mapping is a tactic that will allow you to empower Ambassadors within existing accounts so that you can work wider and deeper to gain even more traction.
- Different from Account Mapping, Account Profiling involves determining the set of characteristics or qualities of an account that help to identify it as a specific type of company.
- The purpose of a meeting is to get another meeting.
- Another way to get Ambassador prospects to respond to you is to be creative in how you tie your solution to your approach.

What I Have as Shown by the Three R's

Resources

Relationships

Reciprocity (How can I give back to my Ambassadors as it relates to this topic?)

What I Need

How I Will Get What I Need

ACTion Step 1

ACTion Step 2

ACTion Step 3

ACTion Step 4

ACTion Step 5

4

Vertical Markets

According to Wikipedia, "a vertical market is a particular industry or group of enterprises in which similar products or services are developed and marketed using similar methods (and to whom goods and services can be sold). Broad examples of vertical markets are: insurance, real estate, banking or financial services, heavy manufacturing, retail, transportation, hospitals, and government. The activities of participants within any given vertical market are typically similar in that they [focus on] solving the same or similar problems. [Companies within a vertical market] are typically competitive because the products and services that are provided to the customers [often overlap]. The single defining characteristic of the participants in a vertical market is competition within a well-defined segment."

The more you target vertical markets, the more expert you will become in those particular industries and the more you'll be able to show how the solutions you provide relate to that market. The benefit of targeting specific industries is that you'll ultimately be viewed as a consultant rather than a salesperson. When working with vertical markets, it is important to understand the benefit your solution brings to the Ambassadors in that particular industry. For example, if you sell customized marketing programs or campaigns and you are working with a high-tech vertical market Ambassador, what are the benefits of your solution as it pertains to high tech? If you're working with the real estate vertical, what are the benefits of your solution as it relates to real estate? If you're working with the financial products vertical, what are the benefits of your solution in the financial products industry, and so on? Once you have a true understanding of the benefits your solution brings to the various vertical markets, you can then do some successful marketing to your potential Ambassadors based on these specific industries.

In Chapter 1, I mentioned writing and leveraging case studies as an effective tool for winning Ambassadors. Prospective Ambassadors will want to know why they should consider working with you, so use this tool to prove your value to an Ambassador. If you organize your case studies by vertical markets, each time you approach a potential Ambassador in a particular industry, you'll be able to show the results you've created for other Ambassadors and customers in that industry. Sharing your success within that industry will cause you to gain immediate credibility with your new Ambassador.

I also discussed Google Alerts in Chapter 1 as well. You can use Google Alerts as an effective tool for tracking what's going on in any given vertical market. Another fantastic resource to track high-tech information specifically as it pertains to the education, health-care, manufacturing, and retail verticals is Network World found online at www.networkworld.com/topics/vertical.html?brl. If you work for a company that is in a high-tech vertical market or you are targeting a high-tech vertical market generally, this Website will be of particular interest to you.

Leveraging Ambassadors in Vertical Markets

In Chapter 3, I talked about First Research (www.firstresearch.com). It's important to mention the company again because its Website is a valuable resource for identifying, working with, and leveraging Ambassadors in both vertical and horizontal markets. First Research provides powerful tools such as "Industry Profiles," "Call Prep Sheets," "Email Alerts," and "State & Province Profiles" that offer a tremendous amount of information to help better prepare you for success in working with Ambassadors in various vertical and horizontal markets.

First Research describes its services this way: "Covering over 200 industries and updated every 90 days, First Research *Industry Profiles* do the 'heavy lifting' for you—saving your sales team valuable research time, enhancing client communications, and giving you the competitive edge to win more business."

First Research profiles help target your products and services directly to prospects. Its profiles provide the information and understanding you need to engage new prospects during the sales process, deepen existing customer relationships, and strengthen your own bottom line.

While it is important to know the facts about certain vertical markets, which you can find by searching First Research industry profiles, before you can decide which potential Ambassadors to pursue, you must first qualify them by considering what vertical markets they represent. It is important to note that some Ambassadors in certain vertical markets may make more sense for you to pursue than others in relation to your overall budget. Some are more likely than others to have set aside funding for your type of product application, as well as the business environment, or culture. Let me explain what I mean in each of these categories.

Companies in some industries are more likely than companies in other industries to always be working within an annual budget cycle. In companies that work with an annual budget, their expenditures are already planned and marked for investments or expenses such as sales and marketing programs, public relations, advertising, and consulting services. If your offering falls into one of the categories in which the companies in a particular vertical market tend to have money set aside for particular purposes, then Ambassadors within those industries are your best vertical markets to pursue. If the amount to cover your offering is already available in a particular company's budget, then it's just a matter of convincing the prospective Ambassadors in that vertical market to promote you based on your merits and the value you bring rather than on what you charge. When pursuing potential Ambassador relationships, as when pursuing any kind of direct prospect for your offering, selling based on the value you bring to the relationship, rather than on price, is always the better way to go.

If, on the other hand, you learn that companies in a particular vertical market generally do not have funds already set aside for your type of offering, it may be better to pursue vertical markets that do. There is enough opportunity out there that it doesn't make sense to spend your time pursuing Ambassadors in a particular vertical market that may not be the best fit anyway. Chances are, if money isn't set aside for your type offering, it will be an uphill battle to gain any traction with potential Ambassadors within that vertical market. Your time is better spent staying focused on those industries that already have the budget earmarked for what you have to offer, and believe me, they're out there if you know where to look.

So where do you find vertical markets that tend to have money set aside for exactly what you have to offer? Take a look at your existing customer base, and determine if a particular vertical market is represented in it. If not, identify the vertical markets your top five customers represent, and ask each of them if he or she had money set aside for your offering before you met. If the customer did, it's likely other companies in the same industry will also have funds earmarked for your type of offering. If not, you may have done such a great job selling the value of what you offer to that customer that it wasn't necessary for him or her to have had the funding set aside in advance. In that case, focus the questions to your customers not on budget but on why else they chose to work with you, and their answers will give you the information you need about the specific value you bring to your customers and to prospective Ambassadors in the same vertical markets. Through a little investigative work on your part, by simply asking questions of your current customers, you will learn a lot about different vertical markets and industries where it makes the most sense for you to pursue potential Ambassadors.

I learned the hard way about vertical markets and whether or not they had the budget for my sales training offering. I pursued the office furniture industry as a vertical market for about a year before realizing that the money to pay for a worthwhile sales training course really wasn't there. While they had some funding earmarked for ongoing education for their dealers, it wasn't enough, and therefore, the dealers were asked to come up with the rest of the budget, which simply wasn't there. I ended up spinning my wheels trying to work within an industry that simply didn't have enough money set aside for sales training. When I finally did find the right vertical markets to work with, such as technology manufacturing companies, it was a no-brainer for prospective Ambassadors to consider working with me because they did have funds available for exactly what I had to offer.

In addition to a budget slated for your offering, another component to consider is the application of your offering within a particular vertical market. The better the fit for your products and services within a particular vertical market, the easier it will be to find Ambassadors to promote you within that specific industry. Again, this goes back to considering your existing customer base and understanding the specific application of your offering within the industries your best customers represent. It will be easy to make a list of potential vertical markets to pursue based on your deciding if there is a general theme of vertical markets that is represented within your customer base, or if there is an industry represented within your top five customers.

In this case, rather than considering budget, you are looking instead for the specific application of your offering within the vertical markets represented within your customer base. Once you have determined a strong application for your offering for a particular customer, it is wise to consider that customer's competitors as prospective Ambassadors, as well as their customers, provided that you don't have an exclusive agreement with each customer based on his or her industry. Once the application for your offering has a proven track record in a specific vertical market, it only makes sense to find other companies within that vertical market that can benefit from your offering in the same way their competitors have.

The final component to consider when pursuing Ambassadors within certain vertical markets is the business environment or culture of that particular industry. For example, if you do workshops on presentation skills and your style is to use humor to engage your audience but a particular vertical market you consider pursuing has a culture that is more serious, that vertical market may not be one you want to pursue. There may, in fact, be a potential conflict between your presentation style and the vertical market's culture, unless, of course, you're willing to change your style to fit within the culture of that particular vertical market. Again, though, there is enough opportunity available that in order to stay focused and seek the best business for you, it would be better to find Ambassadors within vertical markets that have a culture that meshes nicely with your style rather than try to change who you are. If you stay true to who you are, you are more likely to attract the kind of Ambassadors that will be compatible and easy to work with.

While qualifying potential Ambassadors is very important in the process of deciding which prospective Ambassadors to track, it is actually even more important to disqualify potential Ambassadors first. This may sound strange, but think about what you do when qualifying a direct prospect. If you are just learning about a new prospect, isn't the first question you ask the one to which the answer might disqualify him or her? In other words, you don't want to spend a lot of time with a prospect who really isn't a prospect after all, right? Why would you spend your time that way when you could instead focus on working with qualified prospects? If, for example, you sell only to customers who have more than 100 employees, wouldn't the first question you ask of a new prospect be, "How many employees do you have?"

Your prospect's answer to this question could immediately disqualify him or her as a client for you, right? If the answer is, "We have 20 employees," then that person isn't a good prospect for your offering. That's exactly why you should ask this question first, right up front, so that you don't find out later, after spending a lot of time courting the prospect, that he or she has only 20 employees and isn't a potential client after all. The same holds true with Ambassador prospects.

> *The activities of participants within any given vertical market are typically similar in that they aim at solving the same or similar problems.*

Horizontal Markets

Horizontal markets, on the other hand, fulfill a given need of a wide variety of industries rather than meeting a specific one. Horizontal markets often attempt to fill enough of the different needs of vertical markets to gain a presence in the vertical markets. Their similar products and services tend to be less of a fit but also less expensive than specialized, vertical market participant solutions. Horizontal markets can be referred to as "industry neutral" because they satisfy the needs of so many different industries, or vertical markets, across the board.

An example of a horizontal market is word processing software because it can be used in a wide variety of industries rather than being specially designed to work for a specific industry. My own The Blitz Experience sales training program is another example of a horizontal market because it applies to numerous industries, although it has great applications within vertical markets as well. The following table illustrates more examples of vertical and horizontal markets.

Vertical Markets	Horizontal Markets
Agriculture	Communications
Education	Customer relationship management
Health care	Field force automation
Hospitality	Field data access
Insurance	Field data analysis
Professional services	Field data collection
Retail	Knowledge management and delivery
Transportation	Inventory management
Warehousing	Sales force automation

Source: Nathan Clevenger, "Think Horizontal, Mobile Strategies for Corporate Functions" (July 2003).

You can also use Google Alerts to learn about horizontal markets, and, as I mentioned above, you can organize case studies into categories according to their horizontal markets, which will give you easy access to that information when you are working with Ambassadors in a particular horizontal market.

Horizontal markets often attempt to meet enough of the different needs of vertical markets to gain a presence in the vertical market.

FREE TOOLS

Go to www.sittiginc.com, click on the *Power Referrals* icon, and download the "Vertical Markets Worksheet" and the "ACTions to Take Worksheet."

Points to Ponder and ACTions to Take

Points to Ponder

- Broad examples of vertical markets are insurance, real estate, banking or financial services, heavy manufacturing, retail, transportation, hospitals, and government.
- When targeting vertical markets, you become an expert in those particular industries as they relate to the solutions you provide, and you are therefore viewed as a consultant rather than a salesperson.
- Horizontal markets are also good companies to target specifically if your product or solution is "industry neutral" and will benefit a variety of vertical markets across the board.
- There are many tools you can use to target both vertical and horizontal markets, including Google Alerts, First Research, and your own case studies.

What I Have as Shown by the Three R's

Resources

Relationships

Reciprocity (How can I give back to my Ambassadors as it relates to this topic?)

What I Need

How I Will Get What I Need

ACTion Step 1

ACTion Step 2

ACTion Step 3

ACTion Step 4

ACTion Step 5

5

Channels

Whether you are a sales professional selling *to* channels or a sales professional working *within* a channel, winning Ambassadors to promote your business will dramatically increase your sales with less time and effort.

Channels versus Vertical Markets

The difference between a channel and a vertical market is that a channel is specific to an organization while a vertical market is a group of organizations specific to an industry. The channel is the organization's way of bringing its products to market and may include resellers, partners, retailers, direct sellers, enterprise sellers, and original equipment manufacturers (OEMs). High-tech companies such as Microsoft, Xerox, and IBM often go to market via channels. Manufacturing is another common industry to go to market via channels.

Whether you are a sales professional selling to channels or a sales professional working within a channel, winning Ambassadors to promote your business will dramatically increase your sales with less time and effort.

Understanding the Role of Ambassadors and Channel Markets

For those of you who represent an organization that *sells through* channels, it's important to better understand how to turn your dealers, resellers, and partners into Ambassadors. If this describes your situation, then read the sidebar "Maximizing Channel Performance" by Greg Nutter. This is an excerpt from an article originally printed in the *Miller Heiman Sales Performance Journal* (December 6, 2007) regarding maximizing channel performance. For anyone not familiar with this publication, it offers senior sales leaders and executives advice and insights to help deliver top-line growth in their organizations. (For more information visit www.millerheiman.com.)

The writer, Greg Nutter, is a principal with Soloquent, Inc., where he provides a wide range of consulting services to companies looking to improve their direct and indirect sales performance in a complex selling environment. With over 25 years of sales, marketing, sales management, and consulting experience, Greg has developed and implemented a wide variety of global strategies and programs aimed at building and enhancing the performance of direct sales, channel sales, telephone sales, and other revenue-enabling relationships. Greg is also an independent sales performance consultant with Miller Heiman, Inc.

Maximizing Channel Performance

By Greg Nutter

There was a time when third-party reseller channels were used primarily for simple sales—and rarely, if ever, for long-cycle, complex, business-to-business sales. But times have changed: Today more suppliers are using channels for complex sales, characterized by multiple buying influences and a high level of perceived risk on the part of the buyer.

As products and services mature, they almost always head toward reseller channels. For example, in the 1950s and '60s, almost all computer technology was sold through direct sales teams, while today much of it is sold through channels. According to Gartner Inc., 70 percent of Global 1000 organizations now sell through third-party channels. In fact, nearly 50 percent of the world's GNP is transacted through indirect channels, and this number is expected to grow to 65 percent by 2010.

The advantages of selling through channels are well-known and include lower distribution costs, greater market coverage, and faster time to market—as well as the opportunity to access a partner's established local presence, investment, expertise and customer base.

Recognizing that a successful channel is critical to continued corporate growth, many suppliers have tried to sell through channels without fully realizing that it requires a management model not too different from direct selling—a model involving structured selling processes, a common language, and a well thought out approach to managing relationships. As Albert Einstein noted, doing the same thing over and over again and expecting different results is the definition of insanity. Similarly, many suppliers try to manage their channels through a transactional buyer-seller model and struggle, year after year, to realize their expectations without asking themselves what needs to change.

We Have Observed Five Main Challenges in Selling through Channels:

1. Reseller Recruitment

For most channel initiatives, partner recruitment is the greatest point of failure, so getting it right often means the difference between program success and a lot of wasted time and money. As the old saying goes, "If you think hiring professionals is expensive, try hiring amateurs." Channel partnering decisions are a case in point, and the consequences of "hiring" the wrong partner can be significant in terms of lost revenues, high support costs, and damaged brand image, to name just a few. In addition, because there's lots of competition for the best reseller partners, having a strong opportunity management process is critical. Failing to manage partner recruitment as a key success factor might get you a few logos for your Website, but it won't land you star performers.

2. Success Management

Managing a business-to-business reseller to success involves much more than product training and quarterly spiffs.

It requires training, mentoring, and support on how to sell your product effectively in a complex sales environment. Many suppliers miss this key fact and assume that if the reseller knows enough about the product, they'll know how to sell it. Success management done properly will enable the reseller to become progressively more successful. Done poorly, revenue won't flow and you'll incur the cost of having to directly manage many of the deals yourself.

3. Effective Communications
Being able to communicate in a common language regarding the status of key opportunities and the state of the sales pipeline is critical to enable the joint development of winning deals and market development strategies. Failure to develop a common framework for such communication results in poor resource allocation, lost deals, and inconsistent revenue performance.

4. Investment Prioritization
Making decisions regarding what to and what not to invest in is a challenging but important component of channel management. Often, such decisions can appear unilateral or arbitrary in nature, which reduces the chances that they'll achieve their goal and can contribute significantly to partner alienation. Without analysis and decision-making processes that encourage transparency and collaboration, the best ideas might not surface, and many channel investments won't deliver the expected return.

5. Relationship Management

Just as the Pareto principle suggests that 80 percent of our revenues and profits often come from 20 percent of our customers, a similar relationship exists within the channel. We regularly depend on these high-performing key partners to make our yearly numbers, and, without [them], our company revenues would surely suffer. In the direct selling world, significant time and energy is spent managing these key customer relationships. In the channel, however, much less attention is paid. Failing to deploy a consistent methodology and process to manage these "high performer" partners is a recipe for disaster.

Poor or inadequate methodologies and processes in any of these areas can introduce significant challenges to overall channel performance.

To overcome these challenges in today's highly competitive B2B environment, suppliers need:

→ Management methodologies, processes, and tools for:
  - Lead generation
  - Partner selection and skills assessment
  - Managing the reseller opportunity and contracting process
  - Managing the on-boarding process
  - Coaching on effective sales strategy

→ A common selling language to facilitate:
  - Joint selling
  - Joint deal strategizing

- Resource allocation
- Pipeline management and revenue forecasting

→ True partnership orientation to:
  - Ensure alignment of your long-term strategies with your partners
  - Develop strategic and tactical initiatives to achieve these goals
  - Gain commitment from partners for revenue goals and sales objectives
  - Provide channel partners the tools and support they need to achieve their revenue targets
  - Minimize competitive vulnerabilities
  - Build partner loyalty

Earlier this year, I was engaged by ACOM Solutions, a leading provider of back-office technology headquartered in Long Beach, Calif., to help develop key methodologies and processes to recruit resellers, launch its sales channels, and manage its channel activity moving forward.

In the past, ACOM unsuccessfully tried selling through channels. Notes General Manager and Senior Vice President Jim Scott, "We did this without much process or planning and it didn't work. In the old days we shotgunned it," he recalls. Today ACOM is taking better aim. Says Scott: "You have to have a well thought out program and the right processes in place that bring value to every point of the sales channel."

Borrowed Brains

In today's competitive B2B environment, more and more complex sales will come through third-party reseller channels. And good, efficient channel management will be a critical success factor for a lot of suppliers who, just a few years ago, were engaged only in direct sales. Outstanding channel performance is a function of careful planning, thoughtful investment, and long-term thinking. Fortunately, suppliers no longer have to rely on years of trial and error. As ACOM and other companies like it have learned, today there are third-party firms with proven methodologies, processes, and tools to help suppliers identify, recruit, onboard, coach, and manage channel partners so they will sell more strategically and effectively.

As Woodrow Wilson once said, "I not only use all of the brains I have, but all I can borrow."

The strategy of going to market to sell products and services via channels is the perfect example of the Ambassador relationship in its truest form. The manufacturer is often solely dependent on the relationships it has with its channel partners, resellers, and/or dealers, all of which can be considered Ambassadors, to promote and sell its products and services to the end user. It's a very practical and profitable approach because rather than hiring hundreds of expensive direct salespeople, the manufacturer empowers those companies and individuals within the channel to sell its products and services to an existing customer base—that is, the customer base of those companies within the channel. As you are learning how to develop these kind of relationships to promote and sell your products and services through Ambassador relationships, the analogy would be to think of yourself as the manufacturer and think of your Ambassadors as your channel of partners, resellers, and dealers who have the power to promote you to the desired end user of your products, services, and solutions. In other words, by empowering your Ambassadors to promote you the way manufacturing companies empower those within their channels to promote them, you will be able to duplicate an already proven model of success.

The advantages of selling through channels are well-known and include lower distribution costs, greater market coverage, and faster time to market—as well as the opportunity to access a partner's established local presence, investment, expertise and customer base.

—Greg Nutter

Managing Channel Conflict

Many years ago, I worked for a Fortune 500 telecommunications company, and I had been working on selling to a particular account for some time. Like many of the prospects I worked with at this time in my career, this particular prospect had several proposals to consider when making a decision to purchase a new phone system for her office. Something that was an ongoing frustration for me as a salesperson working directly for the manufacturer was the channel conflict that occurred from time to time. So what is channel conflict? Channel conflict takes place when a prospect you're working with has multiple proposals on the table from various dealers or resellers who all represent the same product or product lines that you do.

According to Wikipedia, "Channel conflict can also occur when there has been over production. This results in a surplus of products in the marketplace. Newer versions of products, changes in trends, insolvency of wholesalers and retailers, and the distribution of damaged goods also affect channel conflict. In this connection a company's stock clearance strategy is of importance."

On this particular occasion, I was midway through the sales process when my prospect let me know she had another proposal on the table for the exact same phone system I was trying to sell, from one of our dealers. So as a salesperson, I was basically competing with my own company, since I represented the direct side of the manufacturer, and I was competing with a *dealer* of the manufacturer who sold the same products I did.

The saving grace in this particular situation was that I had developed a business relationship with my prospect that was solid enough that she told my boss she wanted to buy from me rather than the dealer who had offered the same proposal. I won the business, but it was not a fun situation to be in, competing with the very company I represented.

I share this story only to demonstrate the importance of winning Ambassadors with prospects so that if you ever are in a situation of channel conflict, you come out on the winning side. I know many companies going to market through multiple channels have worked on reducing the occurrence of channel conflict by offering products with slight differences that are sold through different channels. So, for example, one phone system sold directly by the manufacturer might be similar to a phone system sold by a dealer, but it would have different features and benefits depending on whether it was purchased directly from the manufacturer or through a dealer. That way, when prospects are comparing two proposals, they are "comparing apples and oranges," as they say, and then it's up to the salespeople to persuade these prospects to buy from them based on the benefits of the products they have to offer.

> ***Channel conflict takes place when a prospect you're working with has multiple proposals on the table from various dealers or resellers who all represent the same product or line of products that you do.***

Leveraging Ambassadors within Channels

The better your relationships, the shorter your sales cycle and the more money you will make.
—Dan Brent Burt

If you work for an organization that goes to market via channels, your potential Ambassadors are those people that represent the aforementioned resellers, partners, retailers, direct sellers, enterprise sellers, and OEMs. If you sell to channels, your potential Ambassadors are those organizations that go to market via channels such as the following high-tech companies—Hewlett-Packard, Microsoft, Xerox, and IBM—as well as manufacturing companies who are also good prospects for finding and leveraging Ambassador relationships.

A great place to find potential Channel Ambassadors is a publication called *VAR Business* magazine published by United Business Media and found online at www.varbusiness.com. *VAR Business* is a *free* publication that offers a plethora of information and strategic insight for technology integrators. The magazine features many companies who go to market via channels, such as value-added resellers (VARs), manufacturers, distributors, wholesalers, and retailers.

The first step is contacting these potential Ambassadors. To help you understand how this Ambassador relationship works, look at the sidebar "Sample Communications with a Channel Ambassador." This is an actual e-mail exchange between one of my Ambassadors, his reseller, and me, and it is an example of how powerful Ambassador relationships can be when you're *selling to* channels.

This particular Ambassador represents a high-tech manufacturing company that goes to market via partners, dealers, resellers, and so on. Ambassador 1, as he's called in this example, had all the tools necessary to promote my business, as discussed in Chapter 1. On this particular occasion, he called to let me know that one of his resellers whom he had told about my training program was interested in moving forward with a program for his sales team.

Sample Communications with a Channel Ambassador

From: Andrea Sittig-Rolf
Sent: Tuesday, November 6, 2007, 3:55 p.m.
To: Ambassador 1
Subject: The Blitz Experience, April 3, 2008
Importance: High

Hi Ambassador 1!

Thanks so much for your call to tell me about your Dallas Reseller's interest in moving forward with a Blitz Experience.

Per our conversation, I have attached the Blitz Agreement and invoice for the Dallas Reseller's Blitz Experience slated for April 3, 2008.

Please ask the Reseller to sign the attached Blitz Agreement and send it along with payment to:

Sittig Incorporated
P.O. Box 2423
Redmond, WA 98073–2423

by no later than 30 days before Blitz day, please, so that we have enough time to prepare and get the reps prepared. Once I receive the signed Agreement and payment, the Reseller's desired Blitz date will be secured on my calendar.

Please let me know if you have any questions.

Thanks Ambassador 1! Looking forward to another great reseller Blitz Experience!

Andrea Sittig-Rolf
The Blitz Master
Sittig Incorporated
T 206–769–4886
www.sittiginc.com

The Blitz Experience . . . are you ready for the magic?

Sittig Incorporated is the creator and exclusive provider of The Blitz Experience, an activity-based sales training program that empowers salespeople to schedule appointments with qualified prospects the day of the training, resulting in a pipeline full of new opportunities at the end of the day!

From: Ambassador 1
Sent: Wednesday, November 7, 2007, 9:19 a.m.
To: Ambassador 1 Reseller
Cc: Ambassador 1 Reseller Contacts
Subject: The Blitz Experience, April 3, 2008
Importance: High

Hi Reseller,
Thanks for agreeing to go ahead with a Blitz Experience event at your office in Dallas on April 3, 2008. This e-mail

is to get the ball rolling so that we're all set to go. I will fund this with Q2 Initiative funds. I'll work with Bob to flow the funding through Reseller HQ and have Bob make payments directly to Andrea at Sittig Incorporated and the list company. I'll send Bob more information on the list company shortly.

A few facts and action items:

1. Training will be Thursday, April 3, 2008, 8 a.m. to 4 p.m. (approx.) at Reseller's Dallas office.
2. Approximately 8 to 10 Reseller sales reps will attend the training.
3. I will be there and hope to have Mike and Barbara join us for joint appointment setting calls.
4. I am getting the list company going on 1,000 commercial midmarket contacts.
5. Can either Bob or Sue please sign and return the agreement to Andrea at Sittig Incorporated?
6. Can Bob proceed to make payment to Sittig Incorporated, delivered no later than February 1, 2008?
7. I will enter funds for payment to Reseller as soon as I receive my Q2 allocation.

If my facts are off or we need to adjust these actions, please let me know and I can update others as appropriate.

Thank you!

Ambassador 1

From: Bob@Reseller
Sent: Wednesday, November 8, 2007, 1:25 p.m.
To: Ambassador 1
Cc: Ambassador 1 Contacts; Ambassador 1 Reseller
Contacts
Subject: The Blitz Experience, April 3, 2008
Importance: High

Hi All,
Please find the signed contract attached.

Thanks!

Bob

Ambassador 1 Reseller

Notice the fast turnaround from the time I received the phone call from my Ambassador, November 6, to the time I received the signed contract from his reseller, November 8. A shortened sales cycle, as this e-mail exchange represents, is just one of the key benefits of the Ambassador relationship. Another benefit is a greater volume of closed deals as a direct result of the number of Ambassadors you are working with who can bring deals to you. And another benefit is the time you save prospecting and hunting for new opportunities because your Ambassadors will do that for you too. As shown in this example, I never spoke or e-mailed with Bob from my Ambassador's reseller until the deal was done and he e-mailed me a signed contract, which was a direct result of my Ambassador's promoting my program, The Blitz Experience, to his reseller.

A shortened sales cycle is just one of the key benefits of Ambassador relationships.

FREE TOOLS

Go to www.sittiginc.com, click on the *Power Referrals* icon, and download the "Channel Ambassadors Map" and the "ACTions to Take Worksheet."

Points to Ponder and ACTions to Take

Points to Ponder

- Today more suppliers are using channels for complex sales, characterized by multiple buying influences and a high level of perceived risk on the part of the buyer.
- Channel conflict takes place when a prospect you're working with has multiple proposals on the table from various dealers or resellers who all represent the same product or product lines that you do.
- A great place to find potential Channel Ambassadors is a publication called *VAR Business* magazine published by United Business Media and found online at www.varbusiness.com.
- Other benefits of Ambassador relationships include (1) a greater volume of closed deals, as a direct result of the number of Ambassadors you are working with who can bring deals to you and (2) the time you save prospecting and hunting for new opportunities because your Ambassadors will do that for you too.

What I Have as Shown by the Three R's

Resources

Relationships

Reciprocity (How can I give back to my Ambassadors as it relates to this topic?)

What I Need

How I Will Get What I Need

ACTion Step 1

ACTion Step 2

ACTion Step 3

ACTion Step 4

ACTion Step 5

6

Social Currency

Imperceptible, yet powerful all the same, social currency is like business accounting for goodwill. People with social currency can move faster and be more effective because they have established trusted relationships.

—Nancy Dailey, Ph.D., and Kelly O'Brien

What Is Social Currency?

Social Currency is the value we bring to the social networks in which we are involved. Think of all of the networks you are involved in; social networks, professional networks, family networks. In every network, you bring value to others in that network based on the people you know and the relationships you have. Social Currency is what you have to "spend" by way of the introductions you make to help the people in your networks get what they want.

Last year I had the incredible opportunity to become one of CanDoGo's first content providers along with Tom Hopkins, Tony Parinello, Zig Ziglar, and other fabulous professional speakers, authors, and trainers. CanDoGo is a provider of Web-based, on-demand, coaching and mentoring solutions. The company converts traditional long-form material into bite-sized advice, known as "CanDoGo Insights," which are delivered through text, audio, and video. Visit CanDoGo at www.candogo.com.

Maximizer Software is one of my clients and the leading provider of simple, accessible, customer relationship management (CRM) solutions. Built on a Web-based architecture, Maximizer CRM offers sales, marketing, and customer service users their choice of access to customer information through the desktop, Web, and mobile devices. Visit Maximizer Software at www.maximizer.com.

As a result of being involved with both companies, I realized what a significant opportunity there was for a mutually beneficial partnership between CanDoGo and Maximizer Software. The press release in the sidebar "Maximizer and CanDoGo Can Do Mentoring" is a result of my introduction of CanDoGo to Maximizer Software and a perfect example of Social Currency.

Maximizer and CanDoGo Can Do Mentoring

The CRM vendor teams up with the business coach to deliver Web-based professional advice through the CRM interface.

Thursday, October 25, 2007

By Marshall Lager

As part of its Global Business Partner Conference 2007, Maximizer Software today announced a partnership with

CanDoGo, a provider of on-demand coaching and mentoring solutions. Under the terms of the exclusive agreement, CanDoGo will provide small and midsize businesses (SMBs) with on-demand sales and professional coaching expertise via Maximizer's CRM interface. The joint offering is scheduled to be generally available beginning in November.

With this new relationship, customers of Vancouver, British Columbia–based Maximizer will have the ability to access advice via the Web from leading experts on business or professional topics such as sales coaching, proposal crafting, leadership, and motivation, according to the companies. The agreement also adds a much-needed live component to Maximizer, which has traditionally provided its on-premise product without Web enhancements.

"Employees within so many organizations wear multiple hats and are faced with numerous constraints. Immediate access to the right information and guidance is critical," said Dave Batt, chief executive officer of Denver-based CanDoGo, in a statement. "Our new partnership with Maximizer delivers expert advice in a new way for SMBs, helping these organizations and their employees improve business execution." Batt, former general manager of CRM for Sage Software, brings his own SMB expertise to the mix along with Maximizer, a company with offerings tightly focused on that market.

CanDoGo has exclusive rights from more than 120 experts to deliver their advice and coaching, including Tom Hopkins, Tony Parinello, Zig Ziglar, [and Andrea Sittig-Rolf] among other authors, speakers, and professional trainers. The company converts traditional long-form material into bite-sized advice, known as "CanDoGo Insights," which are delivered through text, audio, and video. Maximizer customers will be able to access these pearls of wisdom directly through the Maximizer Enterprise CRM software interface.

"The real winners in this new partnership are the sales and business professionals who use Maximizer," said Peter Callaghan, Maximizer's chief sales officer, in a statement. "The most significant barrier to a salesperson's productivity is the lack of access to relevant, best-practices information. Now they will have it on demand, exactly when they need it."

The Maximizer-CanDoGo partnership continues a CRM trend of providing capabilities to smaller businesses that don't have the resources or staff to specialize their job functions. "SMBs don't have a lot of IT expertise, or necessarily even business expertise," says Laurie McCabe, vice president for SMB insights and business solutions at AMI-Partners. The addition of CanDoGo's coaching content "definitely fills a gap," she says. "Companies might send people to one-day training sessions, but they don't usually get serious development time."

The partnership makes good sense for both companies, according to McCabe. "It's definitely a happy partnership; Maximizer gets to add additional value to its CRM product, and CanDoGo gets a springboard," she says. "This joint offering has great market opportunity, particularly because it's offered in conjunction with a CRM interface that professionals are already using every day."

The beautiful thing about this new partnership is the win-win-win it represents. That is to say: CanDoGo, Maximizer, and I all benefit from this partnership. CanDoGo benefits from the ability to leverage the relationships Maximizer has with its customer base by becoming a value-added offering for Maximizer, thus empowering Maximizer as CanDoGo's Ambassador. Maximizer enjoys the ability to offer the robust, content-rich information that CanDoGo provides, without putting forth the time, energy, or expense to develop the CanDoGo platform. I benefit because my content is included on the CanDoGo Website, and in offering to Maximizer customers, I'm now able to reach prospects I may not have been able to reach in any other way. In this case, both CanDoGo and Maximizer are my Ambassadors. In addition, the end users of both CanDoGo and Maximizer enjoy the benefit of easily accessible value-added content in a one-stop-shop format.

In every network, you bring value to others in that network based on the people you know and the relationships you have.

Assessing Social Currency

So how do you determine your Social Currency? Think of all of your spheres of influence: the people you know and the networks you're involved in. Your spheres of influence can include colleagues, associates, referral partners, prospects, customers, friends, family, and Ambassadors. The Social Currency Assessment in the sidebar will help you map and understand your individual strengths and how they can benefit those in your spheres of influence, your potential Ambassadors, and your actual Ambassadors.

Spheres of Influence

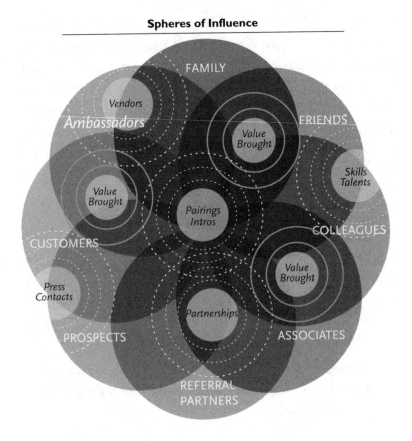

Everyone has skills, abilities, and gifts, and this assessment will help you hone yours for a clear understanding of what strengths you have and what assets you bring to the table in your Ambassador relationships. It's best to simply *manage* those skills and strengths you feel you don't have—that is, your weaknesses—while *building* on those skills and strengths you feel you do have. You can learn more about understanding your own strengths by reading a fantastic book on this topic: *Now, Discover Your Strengths* by Marcus Buckingham and Donald O. Clifton, Ph.D. (Free Press, 2001). This book, which is based on a Gallup study of over 2 million people, reveals 34 common strengths the authors targeted in their research.

Your spheres of influence and your strengths are just part of your overall Social Currency. The other components that make up Social Currency are included in the Social Currency Assessment. Fill in the blanks of the assessment below. Once complete, you will have a better understanding of your Social Currency and the value you bring to your Ambassadors—meaning, what's in it for them to know and work with you.

Social Currency Assessment
Spheres of Influence

Colleagues

1. _____
2. _____
3. _____

- Value I bring to my colleagues

_____

_____

_____

Associates

1. _____
2. _____
3. _____

- Value I bring to my associates

_____

_____

_____

Referral Partners

1. _____
2. _____
3. _____

- Value I bring to my referral partners

_____

_____

_____

- Referrals I can provide

1. _____
2. _____
3. _____

Prospects

1. _____
2. _____
3. _____

- Value I bring to my prospects

_____

_____

_____

Customers

1. _____
2. _____
3. _____

- Value I bring to my customers

_____

_____

_____

Friends

1. _____
2. _____
3. _____

- Value I bring to my friends

_____

_____

_____

Family

1. _____
2. _____
3. _____

- Value I bring to my family

_____

_____

_____

Ambassadors

1. _____
2. _____
3. _____

- Value I bring to my Ambassadors

_____

_____

_____

Skills and Talents

1. _____
2. _____
3. _____

Press Contacts

For example, newspapers, magazines, radio, and TV.

1. _____
2. _____
3. _____

Partnerships

1. _____
2. _____
3. _____

Vendors

1. _____
2. _____
3. _____

Pairings and Introductions

Who do you know that could benefit from knowing each other?

1. _____/_____
2. _____/_____
3. _____/_____

Priority Skills

1. When considering your skills and/or talents, what three things do you think you do best?

   - _____
   - _____
   - _____

2. Which of all of your skills and/or talents are good enough that others would hire you to do them?

   - _____
   - _____
   - _____

6. What additional skills and/or talents do others say that you have that are not yet listed?

   - _____
   - _____
   - _____

10. Great things others have said about you (that is, testimonials).

- _____

- _____

- _____

Everyone has skills, abilities, and gifts, and this assessment will help you hone yours for a clear understanding of what strengths you have and what assets you bring to the table in your Ambassador relationships.

Determining Your Ambassador's Social Currency

Once you have developed good relationships with your Ambassadors, share the results of your Social Currency Assessment with them and ask them to take the Social Currency Assessment and share their results with you. Do this with everyone you feel you bring value to in your sphere of influence. Before you know it, the relationships you have will bloom into mutually beneficial business you never thought possible. It's amazing what can happen to your business with just a little effort, energy, and intention.

About 17 years ago when I was working for a voice-mail services company, I partnered with one of my best Ambassadors who represented a long-distance services company, and we put together what I call a "Mutual Endorsement Mailer."

A Mutual Endorsement Mailer is a marketing tool used not only to promote each other's businesses but to actually make personal introductions for each other. Here's how it works. Review your contact database with your Ambassadors and determine which of your contacts best fits your Ambassadors' Ideal Client Profiles. Next, on *your* letterhead, have your Ambassadors write letters to the contacts in your database who have been identified as fitting your Ambassadors' ICPs to personally introduce your Ambassadors to your contacts. Your Ambassadors are writing letters on your letterhead, as if the letters were coming from you, as a way of being personally introduced to specific contacts in your database.

By having your Ambassadors write the letters, they will be able to stress the key points they want to convey to those receiving the letters. When you write the letters, be sure to include in the package you send any marketing materials that are relevant to your Ambassadors' businesses, as well as your business card and your Ambassadors' business cards. Remember, you should sign the letters because they are coming from you.

Then, have your Ambassadors do the same for you, on their letterhead, with their signature, introducing you to the contacts in their database that fit your ICP. About a week after you send out the mailers, call the contacts to whom you sent them. When you call, say, "I'm calling to follow up on the letter you received from Bob Jones" ("Bob Jones" being your Ambassador). From there, the conversation should flow fairly smoothly, and you now have a great introduction to a new opportunity. What you may find, as my Ambassador and I did, is that you will actually get phone calls from the prospects who received the Mutual Endorsement Mailer before you have a chance to follow up with them!

Once you have developed good relationships with your Ambassadors, share the results of your Social Currency Assessment with them, and ask them to take the Social Currency Assessment and share their results with you.

Leveraging Social Currency to Win Ambassadors

When attending networking events, do you ever notice that there is an overwhelming cloud of "give me" that's in the air? That all the people you meet, while polite in asking what you do for a living, are really just waiting to tell you what they do so you can give them a lead or referral? Ever feel like you're in a room full of salespeople all with something to sell but with no one to buy? Have you been guilty of this common, yet ineffective form of networking? I encourage you to read on and then take the networking challenge and find a few good leads . . . *for someone else.*

The fundamental reason the typical networking process is somewhat unproductive is that all of the people involved are looking for what they can get instead of what they can give. Ironically, giving actually encourages giving more than taking does. In other words, it's human nature to want to give back when someone has given to us. This is the *Rule of Reciprocity* discussed in Chapter 1.

Recently I met with someone with whom I exchange leads on a regular basis. I made a point to focus on only the leads that I could give her that would help grow her business rather than focusing on what leads I might get in return. After listening intently to exactly the type of customer she was looking for, I was able to give her three solid leads. Not only has she closed one of the leads so far, since our meeting she has also given me two leads that have both turned into new customers for me.

The point is that your purpose for networking should be to genuinely help others. So be sure to listen to their specific needs. That said, I encourage you to take the networking challenge.

Write down the name of someone with whom you network on a regular basis. Knowing what type of customer he or she is seeking, look through your database of prospects, customers, and other contacts to determine who in your database might be a good contact for your networking partner. Write down three contacts in your database you think your networking partner would like to meet. Next to each, write a brief synopsis of why you think the contact would be a particularly good candidate for your networking partner to know.

Once you have done this, call your networking partner and share the information you've just written. If it makes sense to do so, introduce your networking partner to the three contacts you have identified, either via e-mail, in a conference call, or in person.

That's it, that's all. Just sit back and wait. Chances are, within a few days, you'll be hearing from your networking partner with some good leads for you.

Applying this same principle, attend the next networking event with a giving attitude and watch what happens. Ask the people you meet what they do for a living and what type of customers they are looking for. As they're answering you, rather than preparing what you're going tell them about your business, try to think of people you know that may be exactly the types of contacts they are looking for.

Challenge yourself to give as many leads as you can, and measure your success at the end of the event not by how many cards you've collected but by how many people you were actually able to help during the event. You may be surprised at the positive outcome this process will have not only in the quality of your networking events and relationships but in the number of additional sales in your own business as well.

A long-time advocate for winning Ambassadors is Sandy Jones-Kaminski, the founder and principal management consultant of Bella Domain. She was often frustrated with the behavior demonstrated by many people at the majority of the networking events she attended as a business development professional. In Chicago, San Francisco, and Seattle, she repeatedly witnessed behaviors from the old "I'm talking to you, but please try not to notice my eyes scanning every other person's name tag that walks by" to the "So, Sandy, what's Bella Domain?" and then the eyes glazing over because she didn't initially appear to be a prospect for them. Sandy recognized that there had to be a better way to make and cultivate meaningful connections, so she started having what are now known as "Pay It Forward Parties," also called "PIF Parties."

The first party invitation went out to about 60 different people that Sandy had met since moving to Seattle, of whom about 30 were able to attend. The only admission request for the gathering was that participants had to be willing to attend with the intention of trying to help at least one other person at the event. The help could be personal (the need for a tip on a car camping location near water) or professional (the need to find a mentor outside a person's own company) or spiritual (the need to find a new religious home on the West Side).

The way Sandy's PIF Parties work is that all the guests come with the intention of helping others first and, as can be expected, the guests leave feeling good about having helped others as well as having been helped themselves. And to keep the momentum going between parties, Sandy has created an online component where people who go to PIF parties can facilitate the follow-up requests that often arise after the events, and, if they choose, they can share outcomes that have occurred because of the connections made at the parties. Please visit www.belladomain.com for more information.

Challenge yourself to give as many leads as you can, and measure your success at the end of the event not by how many cards you've collected but by how many people you were actually able to help during the event.

FREE TOOLS

Go to www.sittiginc.com, click on the *Power Referrals* icon, and download the "Social Currency Assessment Template," "the Social Currency Assessment Spheres of Influence Diagram," the "Mutual Endorsement Mailer Template," and the "ACTions to Take Worksheet."

Points to Ponder and ACTions to Take

Points to Ponder

- Social Currency is the value we bring to the social networks in which we are involved.
- The Social Currency Assessment will help you map and understand your individual strengths and how they can benefit those in your spheres of influence, your potential Ambassadors, and your actual Ambassadors.
- Once you have developed good relationship with your Ambassadors, share the results of your Social Currency Assessment with them, and ask them to take the Social Currency Assessment and share their results with you.
- Take the networking challenge and find a few good leads . . . *for someone else.*

What I Have as Shown by the Three R's

Resources

Relationships

Reciprocity (How can I give back to my Ambassadors as it relates to this topic?)

What I Need

How I Will Get What I Need

ACTion Step 1

ACTion Step 2

ACTion Step 3

ACTion Step 4

ACTion Step 5

7

Self-Promotion

Authentic self-promotion is grounded in the conviction that you have something of unique value to offer the world and that you are willing to discover how to embody that offer, to show up and serve, and to thrive in the process.

—Molly Gordon

When you own your own company or are a sales professional, you are ultimately in the business of self-promotion, and the ability to promote yourself can make or break your business. Some people are concerned with crossing the fine line between confident self-promotion and seeming arrogant. But keep in mind that shameless self-promotion is the only way to get people to know about you and your business. The suggestions given in this chapter are my secrets for using self-promotion to your advantage without crossing that line.

Newsletters

Newsletters are more than a great way to stay in touch with your Ambassadors; they're also a great way to stay top-of-mind with them too. The key to effective newsletters is to provide value and not to just try to sell something or run a promotion each time. Determine what's valuable to your Ambassadors as it pertains to your expertise, and then write about it. By doing this on a regular basis, monthly, for example, you stay in the forefront with them, and they will be likely to think of you when an opportunity to work together arises.

The sidebar "Sample Newsletter" is an example of a newsletter I recently mailed to my Ambassadors. In addition to providing the template to give you a sense of length and focus, I also hope that you will get something from the content too.

Sample Newsletter

How to Plan a Successful Sales Call

By Andrea Sittig-Rolf

"If you fail to plan, you plan to fail." That's an old saying, and it's essentially what you're doing if you go into any meeting cold without properly preparing. You don't have to be the formal type to have a plan. Every salesperson should have a plan going into any meeting with a new prospect, long-time customer, or anyone in between. The plan doesn't have to be complicated, but it should cover a few key points.

First, start with the big picture, also known as "the 50,000-foot view." Consider the following questions, and write down the answer to each one as a way to help you gather your thoughts before your meeting:

What is the purpose of your meeting? What do you want to accomplish? What is your goal? What do you know about the prospects specifically? What do you know about their industry? What do you know about the company? What is left to learn about the prospects? What are the prospects' expectations of your meeting? What do the prospects want to accomplish? What is the next step after your meeting?

While I don't recommend going into the meeting with this list of questions and answers in front of you, if you write them down and provide the answers before your meeting, they will stay fresh in your mind so you are fully prepared. In doing so, it will be obvious to your prospects, and they most likely will appreciate that you took the time to prepare for your meeting.

Next, after determining the big picture of your meeting, or the general scope of what you want to accomplish, be prepared to ask the following questions of your prospects, keeping in mind the open-ended nature of each:

Tell me about your company. Help me understand your personal goals regarding your role at the company. Tell me about your plans [regarding the area where your solution may be of benefit]. Are you working with other providers regarding a solution similar to the one we might provide? If so, who? What do you like about them? What areas of their products, services, or solutions could be improved? Give me an idea of what would be ideal in terms of working with a provider of the solution we're here to discuss. Tell me a little bit about your decision-making process. Who is involved in making the decision? Do you have information regarding your current solution that I could take a look at? How do you envision our working together? If you decide to move forward, what is it you would like to accomplish with the solution we provide?

In addition to knowing what questions to ask, it is important that you know what questions you may be asked to answer, such as the following:

→ What are your rates? (Or, how much is it?) *Answer:* We have lots of programs and/or packages.

→ Tell me a little more about your strategy and plans for. . . . Who else have you done business with in our industry? What were the results your solution created for them? *Answer:* I'd be happy to share several case studies that speak to the results we've created for our other clients. (Be prepared to share them.)

→ What is your process for delivery? *Answer:* Share your process.

→ What can I expect in terms of service? *Answer:* Elaborate on the service your company provides, and give examples of your level of service.

→ Who else on your team might I be working with if I choose to buy from you? *Answer:* Share the names and roles of others on your team who would be involved in the project.

→ What is my recourse if I am unsatisfied with the solution you provide? *Answer:* Let them know your return, exchange, or guarantee policy.

→ Tell me what you know about our company. *Answer:* Share what you know based on the research you did in preparation for the meeting.

→ Why should I choose to work with you instead of your competition? *Answer:* Explain the benefits provided by you and your solution without bashing the competition. Focus on your strengths, not the competition's weaknesses.

These questions will give you an idea of how to approach your first meeting. Keep the dialogue going by asking open-ended questions, encouraging your prospect to do most of the talking. Answer questions thoroughly, and if you're not sure why the person is asking a particular question, don't be afraid to ask why so you know how to better answer it.

One final thought is to remember that the purpose of a meeting is to schedule another meeting. Doing so will help you move your prospect through the sales process until it just makes sense to do business together.

Happy Selling!
Andrea Sittig-Rolf

Newsletters can be sent via e-mail or standard mail, but I prefer e-mail because it gives your Ambassadors an opportunity to reply to your newsletter immediately. What often happens is that Ambassadors will reply with an actual opportunity for you that has nothing to do with the topic you wrote about in the newsletter. The reason is that you've sent them an e-mail, and that has reminded them that you're out there and available to work with. The online service I use to send my e-mail campaigns is called Constant Contact, and they can be found online at www.constantcontact.com. They offer a great service that's easy to use, can be customized to match your branding, and is quite cost effective.

Newsletters aren't just a great way to stay in touch with your Ambassadors; they're also a great way to stay top-of-mind with them too. The key to effective newsletters is to provide value and not to just try to sell something or run a promotion each time.

Newsletter Contributions

In addition to providing your own monthly newsletters, a fantastic way to promote your business is what I call *newsletter contributions*. There are two types of newsletter contributions. The first happens when your clients or Ambassadors are so happy with the services you provide that they offer to include a write-up about your service in their internal company newsletter. If you do a great job for your clients and Ambassadors, they'll want others to know about it because it makes them look good to be associated with you and the work you've done for them. Also, if the work you've done for particular clients or Ambassadors is helpful to them, they'll want others in their company to know about it because it may be just as helpful for them. The sidebar "Sample Newsletter Contribution" is an example of this type of newsletter; this particular contribution came from one my clients called SunSource, a company based in Addison, Illinois, and it was written by my Ambassador Tom Kennedy, who is the vice president of human resources.

Sample Newsletter Contribution

Excerpt from the SunSource Quarterly Newsletter, Issue 11, December 2007

By Tom Kennedy, Vice President of Human Resources, SunSource

If you are an account manager (AM) who struggles in scheduling appointments with prospective customers, what are you to do? Recently 37 of our AMs had the opportunity to add a few new tools to their toolbox, and they wasted no time in putting them to good use! These AMs attended a new SunSource University–sponsored course called "The Blitz Experience," and during this one-day training session, over 300 appointments with prospective customers were made! While there is nothing magical about it, the fundamental techniques presented show you how to accomplish the following:

→ How to get past gatekeepers
→ How to overcome common objections and get the appointment

→ How to leave effective voice-mail messages that get a
   response
→ How to increase connections with decision makers
   leading to more appointments, leading to more sales

The Blitz Experience is an energy-packed day of prac-
ticing sales techniques, regrouping and sharing experiences,
and then getting back on the phone to practice some more
(usually "stealing" great ideas from our peers!). Andrea
Sittig-Rolf, The Blitz Master, brings years of experience in
sales and sales training, as well as enough energy to power
any engine!

We all know the importance of tracking our results, and
this training provides a simple way to determine the ROI!
During the training, participants are tracking calls, con-
nects, appointments, voice-mails, returned voice-mails, and
no's. Because of SASS and its capabilities, we will be tracking the number of orders that come from these appointments. Already AMs are getting orders as a direct result of
The Blitz Experience!

Don't be shy; ask your fellow AMs who have attended
The Blitz Experience to share the success they have had with
these tools. The participant feedback has been extremely
positive, and the ultimate value of the training will be realized as the orders keep coming in!

Tom Kennedy
Vice President of Human Resources, SunSource

The second type of newsletter contribution occurs when *you write* an article or column for your clients' or Ambassadors' internal company newsletters. Again, by writing something of value that's pertinent to your expertise and their businesses, you make it easy for your Ambassadors to include your information in their newsletters, which in turn, promotes your business. Sometimes you're actually doing them a favor because it can be difficult for them to come up with new content for each newsletter they write. It's sharing Social Currency, as we discussed in Chapter 6.

If you're able to contribute one article to your Ambassadors' newsletters, that's great, but creating a column that's published in every newsletter they issue is even better! The sidebar "Sample Client Newsletter" provides an example of a column I provide for the AB Corporation's monthly newsletter. The premise is that readers write to me with their sales dilemmas, and I answer them via the column.

Sample Client Newsletter

Excerpt from the AB Corporation Newsletter: "Sales Tools"

By Andrea Sittig-Rolf

While it is important to "do the numbers," because sales is a numbers game, you can improve your numbers and success ratios by improving your skills around prospecting phone calls. The most important skill you can learn to help improve your success ratios when making prospecting phone calls is how to overcome the common objections you will hear when asking for the first appointment with new prospects. I have developed the Aha! formula, a formula that works extremely well for overcoming common objections you should expect to hear when calling new prospects for the first time.

The Aha! formula is simply to *anticipate* the objection, *handle* the objection, and *ask* for the appointment: Aha!

The first key to success when using the Aha! formula is to anticipate or expect that you will get objections to your request for an appointment. If you anticipate that you will hear objections, you will be ready for them and you will be prepared to handle them. If you do not anticipate the objections, you will be thrown by them and probably stumble and say something like, "Okay, thanks for your time," and hang up the phone—only to make the next call and go through the same thing again.

Instead, after you've asked for the appointment, get ready to hear "no" in some shape or form. Prepare in advance the way you will handle it when propects say "no" to your request for an appointment. Here are some suggestions on how to do that:

→ You know, Mr. Prospect, that's exactly what ABC Company said until it realized . . . [describe a result you've created for another client].

→ That's exactly why we should meet in person, so I can learn more about your company to determine if there's a fit for my services.

→ My services will actually complement what you're already doing.

Now that you've handled the objection, it's crucial you do the final part of the Aha! formula, and that is to ask for the appointment. Immediately following your response to the prospect's objection, ask for the appointment by saying something like, "How's Thursday at 10 a.m.?"

Be specific when you ask for the appointment rather than giving a choice such as "How's Tuesday morning or Thursday afternoon?" I recommend this for a couple of reasons: One, you want to make it as easy as possible for your prospects to decide when they can meet with you. By offering several options, it complicates the process by requiring your prospects to look in several different spots on their calendar.

Also, asking for a specific date and time lets prospects know you are busy too and that "Thursday at 10 a.m." works in your calendar. If a prospect says, "No, that doesn't work for me," then all you're talking about is what time and date will work to meet for an appointment, rather than if you should meet at all.

Now, let's put it all together.

After you've asked for the appointment, your prospect says "no."

You have anticipated the objection and you're ready for it. Now, handle the objection: "You know, Mr. Prospect, that's exactly what ABC Company said until they realized . . . [result of your solution]. [Now, ask for the appointment:] "Why don't we just get together Thursday at 10 a.m.?" [Notice the

Aha! formula: anticipate the objection, handle the objection, ask for the appointment.]

Here are some additional tips:

→ Don't overcome more than three objections per call. If a prospect gives you three objections, use the Aha! formula to overcome them all; however, after the fourth objection, thank the prospect for his or her time and then hang up. You don't want to argue with the prospect because, after all, sometimes the answer is "no!"

→ Should a prospect ask you to call back at another time to set the appointment, try this: "Why don't we tentatively put something on the calendar now, and I'll call back to confirm? How's Thursday at 10 a.m.?" Studies show that once an appointment is on the calendar, there is a 70 percent greater likelihood it will occur, even if it's "tentative." So if you can get your prospect to put you on the calendar, there is a good chance the appointment will happen. The chances of your getting that prospect back on the phone again at a later time are slim to none.

Try the Aha! formula the next time you're prospecting for new business over the phone. You will not only increase your telephone prospecting skills and set more appointments but you will also ultimately win more customers and close more sales.

There's nothing wrong with self-promotion, especially in cases in which it helps your clients and Ambassadors. Offer to provide newsletter contributions to your clients and Ambassadors and see what happens. If you've got a solid relationship with them and they're happy with the work you do, they'll gladly take you up on it.

> *By writing something of value that's pertinent to your expertise and their businesses, you make it easy for your Ambassadors to include your information in their newsletters, which in turn, promotes your business.*

Press

There is no such thing as bad publicity except your own obituary.
—*Brendan Behan*

Shortly after I started my business in May 2002, it occurred to me that publicity, in terms of print and radio, was going to be an important way to promote my business, especially given the limited budget I had for advertising. I also realized that getting an article published about my company would be much more effective, in terms of self-promotion, than paying for advertising. Of course, there is a certain amount of risk associated with getting publicity. Unlike advertising you pay for, when other people write about your company, they determine the message and you have very little say about the final draft. Keeping this in mind, I still decided to pursue the publisher of a well-known sales magazine that includes content directed at sales professionals, which was my target audience.

After years of contacting a particular publisher and being politely rejected, but rejected nonetheless, I was finally able to convince him to include a story about my company in an edition of the magazine. He then had a writer call to interview me, and as a result, an extremely well written, four-page article was published. I was over the moon because I knew this article was going to lead to some business for me. Sure enough, a month or so after the article was published, I was contacted by the VP of sales of one of North America's leading power distribution companies who inquired about my training program. As a direct result of this article, the prospect signed up and has become one of my largest clients to date!

In addition to the leads and inquiries that come in as a result of press like this, by ordering reprints of published articles, you have a fantastic tool to include in your Ambassador Toolkit that will allow your Ambassadors to share the articles with others who are candidates for your offerings. Also, get electronic versions of the articles to include on your Website so that you can share them in the form of attachments to the e-mails you send to Ambassadors.

Although you don't have as much control when publications write about you as you do when you pay for advertising, articles written by others about your company add credibility to your offering.

Think about the trade magazines in circulation that relate to your topic of expertise, and consider contacting them to determine their interest in writing articles about your company. Most trade publications provide contact information to their readers for this very purpose.

Press releases are something you can create yourself, and they can be a great way to promote your business. A powerful Website that provides information on how to do this, as well as distribution services, is PR Web Press Release Newswire, found online at www.prweb.com. PR Web allows you to share your news with the world in just three easy steps:

1. Create a free account in minutes.
2. Upload your release and any additional files, and use the search engine optimization (SEO) tools to ensure maximum online visibility.
3. Submit your release, and PR Web does the rest.

You'll also have the ability to track your release once it has been created and sent.

Local newspapers are often looking for stories to write about when they need additional content to fill the pages of their publications. Five years ago when I started Sittig Incorporated, I also started a company called ParoDiva Productions, a company that created customized parodies to perform at corporate events. The premise was that I would interview the employees of the clients that hired me to learn about their culture, the people, and any fun customs or traditions that were a part of their organization. I would then write about their customs and culture, and sing what I had written to a popular tune at events such as Christmas parties, corporate sales meetings, and employee recognition parties. The concept was unique, so after sending out a press release about my new company, through PR Web as mentioned above, I was contacted by a local newspaper who was interested in doing an in-depth story about it. To my surprise, what resulted from my interview with the paper was a full-page article called "Party performer has song for you," and the article included a color photograph of me belting it out. This publicity created a deluge of inquiries from local radio stations and other publications, and it was the best free advertising I could have asked for.

Radio is another source of publicity that can be very powerful in terms of self-promotion. Like many publications, radio shows often need content, and they are very open to providing content based on the expertise of someone in the field that relates to the topic being presented. If you are a sales professional, for example, a couple of radio shows that are particularly relevant are *Sales Talk with Russ Lombardo* and *Sales Rep Radio to Go*. Other radio shows that include many different business topics include the *eWomen Network Radio Show*, and *Alternative Talk Radio 1150 AM KKNW*. Most radio producers are more than willing to give you a copy of your radio interview to include on your Website. You can also Google "business talk radio online" for even more information about this topic.

Still another popular press medium is video. A couple of years ago I had the pleasure of meeting Gerhard Gschwandtner, founder and publisher of *Selling Power* magazine. After explaining The Blitz Experience to him and asking for his suggestions on how to get my name out to the media and potential Ambassadors, he had the brilliant idea of creating a short video as a way of showcasing my company.

I worked with him to create a professionally produced, five-minute video that included an interview with him asking me questions about The Blitz Experience and footage from an *actual* presentation I did for a client in New York City. Not only did this video provide the perfect medium to highlight the true benefits of my program, it also became the single most effective self-promotional tool in my arsenal, because prospective clients and Ambassadors could see me in action to better understand the concept of what I was offering and the kind of results it can produce.

In addition to providing the video link to Ambassador prospects to promote my business, the video that resided on the

Selling Power Website generated tens of thousands of dollars in revenue from new clients who saw the video online. If you're looking to do a *professional* video for your business that will create a lasting impression on your Ambassadors, contact *Selling Power* to learn more about how to put one together for your business. The company can be reached at www.sellingpower.com.

The key to self-promotion is that you can't sit back and wait for publications and radio shows to contact you. To be effective, you must be proactive in your approach. I'll get in to this a little more in the next chapter.

Although you don't have as much control when publications write about you as you do when you pay for advertising, articles written by other people about your company add credibility to your offering.

Contests

Have you ever thought of entering a contest to win an award for your business? Imagine what awards and trophies can do to promote your business. Business awards represent recognition from your peers, show excellence in what you do, and can be very powerful self-promotional tools. A popular contest in the sales industry is the Selling Power Sales Excellence Award presented by Stevie Awards, found online at www.stevieawards.com. All sales professionals, teams, and organizations worldwide are eligible to be nominated for the Selling Power Sales Excellence Awards.

Another popular business contest is called "40 Under 40," and it is sponsored by the American City Business Journals, which have local publications in over 40 markets across the country.

They can be found online at www.bizjournals.com. The 40 Under 40 contest takes place once a year, and it spotlights the next generation of business leaders. They look for people under the age of 40 who work hard to drive the business community's future and demonstrate dynamic leadership and social responsibility. Receiving this award will go far in promoting not only your business, but also you personally and what you bring to the table for your Ambassadors and other business relationships.

Any time you write a newsletter or contribute to a newsletter, are recognized positively in the press, do a radio interview, or win an award or contest, include it on your Website. Create a section that is specially designed for "newsletters," and creat another one for "press/news/radio." Post any awards that you win directly on your home page for visitors to see immediately when logging on. Visitors to your Website, as well as Ambassadors and prospective clients, are usually interested first and foremost in what you've accomplished and what results you've achieved for others. Giving them the opportunity to see this kind of information immediately establishes the credibility you need so that others feel comfortable working with you.

> *Business awards represent recognition from your peers, show excellence in what you do, and can be very powerful self-promotional tools.*

FREE TOOLS

Go to www.sittiginc.com, click on the *Power Referrals* icon, and download the "Press Release Checklist," the "Newsletter Template," and the "ACTions to Take Worksheet."

Points to Ponder and ACTions to Take

Points to Ponder

- When you own your own company or are a sales professional, you are really in the business of self-promotion, and the ability to promote yourself can make or break your business.
- The key to effective newsletters is to provide value and not to just try to sell something or run a promotion each time.
- By writing something of value that's pertinent to your expertise and their businesses, you make it easy for your Ambassadors to include your information in their newsletters, which in turn, promotes your business.
- In order to be effective, you must be proactive in your approach.
- Business awards represent recognition from your peers, show excellence in what you do, and can be very powerful self-promotional tools.

What I Have as Shown by the Three R's

Resources

Relationships

Reciprocity (How can I give back to my Ambassadors as it relates to this topic?)

What I Need

How I Will Get What I Need

ACTion Step 1
ACTion Step 2
ACTion Step 3
ACTion Step 4
ACTion Step 5

8

Winning Ambassadors in the Press

Social media generally frowns on self-promotion, in many cases admonishing outright those who practice it. But with the sheer numbers of new videos, posts, sites, pictures, and stories appearing each and every day, self-promotion is a necessity for anyone starting out and hoping to gain any sort of foothold.

—Matthew Peters, from Blogging, Advice and Tips, Social Media

Newspapers, Magazines, and Trade Journals

Being quoted by the press is one of the most powerful methods of free advertising because it helps to establish that you are an expert in your field. To be fortunate enough to receive this form of free advertising, you must first know how to present your business, or your story, as newsworthy. Editors and reporters are always looking for good content, so learning how to present your material in such a way that helps editors or reporters do their job better and easier will allow you to win them over as Ambassadors—Ambassadors who are in a position to help get your information to the masses.

Before pitching your ideas to newspapers, magazines, and trade journals, first create a one-page biography that includes all pertinent information about your background and your expertise. What journalists care about most when working with you for the first time is why you are the one to write the article or column you're pitching. In other words, what makes you the expert on this particular topic? Do your research on the publication ahead of time to understand the audience of the column if you're pitching an article to be included in the column, or the audience for the newspaper if you're pitching an idea for a new column.

Believe it or not, pitching your ideas to publications, or even radio and TV shows, does not have to be a daunting task. Most journalists as well as radio and TV producers are actually looking for good content. It can be tough for them to fill pages of a publication or to fill air time without the help of professionals just like you. Don't be shy about reaching out to people in the media with your ideas. You might be surprised with how well you are received. The key is to reach out in a way that is welcomed by the press.

Most journalists and editors do not like to receive an entire article to consider for publication but instead prefer to receive a query. A query is a short pitch of your idea. By sending them a query, you (a) save the editors' time in reading an entire article they may not be interested in, and (b) save your time in writing an article that perhaps no one is interested in publishing.

Mui Tsun, the creator of Inspire Software, which is a software program designed to kick-start your imagination and clear your writer's block, has some fabulous tips for sending queries to magazines that will also be effective when pitching queries to newspapers and trade journals. The following are her 10 steps for writing a magazine query:

1. Get the editor's and publication's names right.
2. Know your audience.
3. A grand opening: Make your opening sentence work for you.
4. Get to the point quickly.
5. Be professional.
6. Be focused.
7. Mail or e-mail, but no phone.
8. Clips, or no clips: Include only those clips of your published work that are pertinent to the topic you are pitching.
9. Learn from your rejections.
10. Give it 100 percent.

For more information, you can find the entire article "10 Steps to a Magazine Query" online at www.freelancewriting.com/articles/ten-steps-to-a-magazine-query.php.

One idea for a column you can pitch to newspapers, magazines, and/or trade journals is a question-and-answer column for which you are the expert to whom readers write for advice concerning dilemmas in your area of expertise; you then answer the readers' questions in the column. I've done this with numerous publications, and it has been a great way not only to get my name out there as sales expert but also to generate leads for my business. There's nothing wrong with writing this type of column for multiple publications as long as the publications don't directly compete with each other and all of the editors of the various publications you're working with know you're doing something similar with other publications. Typically you won't be paid for this type of work, but you will reap a substantial benefit in the long run in terms of both intangible and tangible gains. For example, an important part of winning Ambassadors, whether they be prospects, customers, or the press, is establishing your credibility as an expert. The activity of writing columns helps to establish credibility because it gives you the chance to get your name out on a regular basis. Seeing your name over and over again, and in multiple publications, will make potential Ambassadors feel comfortable working with you without your having to do a sales pitch to convince them.

Believe it or not, pitching your ideas to publications, or even radio and TV shows, does not have to be a daunting task. Most journalists as well as ratio and TV producers are actually looking for good content.

Online Press

Even if you are unsuccessful in getting your content published in newspapers, magazines, or trade journals, there is the whole world out there we call the "World Wide Web" that allows you to share your content with the world, and you don't even need anyone's permission!

Blogs are a perfect example of a way to share your content online. A blog is a Website that displays in chronological order the postings by one or more individuals, and it usually has links to comments on specific postings. Just do a search for the word "blog" and see how many hits come up: almost 2 billion! This has obviously become a popular way to communicate online. You'll also see many sites that guide you through setting up your own blog if you don't already have one.

Creating a press and news section on your Website allows you to post all of the news about your business, and it is another way for both the press and for potential Ambassadors to learn more about you and your company. What is especially compelling about a press and news section on a Website is the history that develops over time. For example, your most recent news will be listed first in this section of a Website, and when potential Ambassadors scroll down, they will see all of the news that came before it. I update the press and news section of my Website about once a month, and after being in business for more than five years now, this section of my Website showcases the history of my company.

> **What is especially compelling about a press and news section on a Website is the history that develops over time.**

Turning Journalists into Ambassadors

Make it as easy as possible for the reporter to cover your story. They do not have the time to track down leads and facts. The more you can complete the story for your journalist friends, the more likely they will do something with your story. Make sure you have an online press room. Have the story, images, graphs, video, key contacts, etc., prepared for the journalists.
—*Green Media Toolshed*

Turning journalists into Ambassadors requires abiding by some specific guidelines to not only get their attention but to stay in their good graces, allowing you the opportunity to continue to work with the press who in turn can promote your business.

Most journalists use a combination of sources and resources for the content of their articles. They may get anywhere from 75 to 250 or more inquiries a week by e-mail, fax, and phone calls. E-mail is generally the way they prefer to receive inquiries, probably because it's easy to sort by topic and because it is easy to respond to the sender by reply e-mail if they are interested in the topic. Try to avoid sending attachments with your e-mail; instead, provide all of your information in the body of the e-mail. Also keep in mind that good timing can often be a huge advantage when contacting a journalist regarding a particular story.

When sending queries to journalists, as in sales, it's important to "do the numbers." This means that when you want to turn journalists into Ambassadors, you must contact enough of them so that you will have sufficient opportunities to pitch your idea and be more likely to contact someone at just the right time. The idea behind doing the numbers is that it practically guarantees you'll eventually reach someone who will give you a shot. Once you begin working with particular journalists, you will then have the opportunity to turn them into Ambassadors by continuing to work with them. Check out the guidelines on each publication's Website to find out exactly what is required to be a contributor to that particular publication.

How many times have you cold called a prospect and been told, "Wow, your timing is impeccable. We were talking about needing your solution just the other day." That probably doesn't happen as often as you'd like, but it's more likely to happen if you call a lot of people, right? So by the same token, send queries to enough journalists and you may just reach someone who happens to be interested in your topic because you've contacted that person at just the right time.

What is and is not perceived as newsworthy will depend solely on the journalists you contact. This is why it's so important to do the numbers and reach out to as many journalists as possible so that you're more likely to reach one who *does* find your pitch newsworthy. Also, even if your pitch is not newsworthy at the time you contact a particular journalist, the journalist may hold on to your query for future reference in the event that your topic does come up as one of interest. So don't feel discouraged if you don't hear back from someone immediately.

Compelling subject lines in the e-mail queries you send are vital to getting the attention of journalists. The subject lines should be truthful and intriguing at the same time. The idea behind effective subject lines is that they persuade the journalists to open your e-mails and actually read them. If the subject lines don't grab their attention, your e-mails will likely be deleted without even being opened. If you're able to provide results or proof to back up your story ideas or pitches, that's even better. Obviously, good writing is of the utmost importance too, so if you don't feel you're a good writer, ask someone to help you.

Paul Lima, a freelance writer and writing coach, writes on his blog, "Instead of opening with, 'Are you interested in an article on . . .,' use your lead to reflect the writing that appears in the magazine or newspaper. For instance, for a consumer-oriented health magazine or the 'life' section of the newspaper, your query might start like this:"

> Is there any truth to the expression "An apple a day keeps the Doctor away"? Yes, and here's the proof. According to the Nutritional Institute of Canada, one apple a day contains the daily-recommended dose of vitamins X, Y, and Z. Apples are also an excellent source of roughage, contain few calories, and make great snacks for kids.

"Such a lead demonstrates that you can write and captures the attention of the editor who, when you think about it, represents the publication's readers."

The key to winning Ambassadors in the press and building strong relationships with them is to stay in touch. Be persistent but also be brief and professional. Checking in about once a month should allow you the opportunity to connect with journalists when they have a need or interest for your particular subject. Don't give up after a couple of pitches if you don't have any luck. Like any other sales process, it takes time and tenacity to win Ambassadors in the press. This is a part of the process that allows your relationships with journalists the time to solidify.

One of the best ways to lose Ambassadors in the press is not to do your homework or research on particular journalists to understand the kind of stories or topics they write about. Over time, if particular journalists continue to receive irrelevant queries from you, they may start to delete your queries as soon as they receive them. It's also important to do the research on your topic before pitching it to journalists so that it's clear to them that you understand the relevance of your topic at the time you are pitching it.

During the course of reaching out to journalists to present your story ideas, you may have the opportunity to be interviewed by the press. Be sure to provide the journalist with an overview of your background, expertise, and topic. Also, listen well and ask questions about the article the journalist has agreed to write, such as the focus of the article, its deadline, its length, and when it will be published. Answers to the journalist's questions should be concise and to the point. He or she can always ask more questions, but it's best to start with the essential facts. Communication is crucial. If a deadline is slipping away from you, send a quick update to the journalist regarding the status and don't make promises you can't keep. As in sales, when dealing with the press, it's always better to underpromise and overdeliver.

In order to keep journalists interested in your topic, your content should be dynamic, but it should also follow a methodology and be factual. Begin with a compelling lead-in and use interesting language. Start from the beginning, and create a clever hook to get their attention, but also continue to deliver the story in a way that's enticing. Don't be too dramatic in your approach, don't lead into your story by making unrealistic or unbelievable claims, and try to avoid clichés that are overused. Just be straightforward with the subject matter and consider whether or not the hook is appropriate.

In order to keep journalists interested in your topic, your content should be dynamic, but it should also follow a methodology and be factual.

FREE TOOLS

Go to www.sittiginc.com, click on the *Power Referrals* icon, and download the "Journalists into Ambassadors Worksheet" and the "ACTions to Take Worksheet."

Points to Ponder and ACTions to Take

Points to Ponder

- What journalists care about most when working with you for the first time is why you are the one to write the article or column you're pitching.
- Remember, when turning journalists into Ambassadors, you must contact enough of them so that you will have sufficient opportunities to pitch your idea and be more likely to contact someone at just the right time.
- If you are interviewed, your answers to the journalist's questions should be concise and to the point.

What I Have as Shown by the Three R's

Resources

Relationships

Reciprocity (How can I give back to my Ambassadors as it relates to this topic?)

What I Need

How I Will Get What I Need

ACTion Step 1

ACTion Step 2

ACTion Step 3

ACTion Step 4

ACTion Step 5

9

Leveraging Ambassadors to Close Business

Have you ever wondered how you could leverage your current customers as Ambassadors to help you close more business? Have you ever asked your current customers to be your Ambassadors and help you close new opportunities? Have you considered that if you have, in fact, created outstanding results for your customers and they're happy with the service you've provided, that they might just be willing to return the favor? Introducing your prospects to happy customers creates a compelling environment for your prospects to decide to do business with you.

To clarify, the difference between this technique of leveraging or empowering Ambassadors to *close* business versus empowering Ambassadors to *promote* your business is that when you leverage them to *close* business, *you* are the one bringing the prospect and current customer together to have a discussion about the services you provide and the outstanding results you create. When empowering Ambassadors to *promote* your business, the Ambassadors are bringing the prospects to you to close.

Let me offer a couple of examples of how this has worked for me. Recently I had an opportunity to present my one-day sales training program to a team of partner business managers for AB

Corporation. The team manages AB Corporation's largest global partner, which I'll call XYZ Company. We started with a conference call to discuss the methodology of my training, logistics, pricing, and other details. We also discussed the one-day sales training programs I've conducted for many AB Corporation channel partners over the last three years. Although the curiosity of the managers was peaked, they were not completely convinced of the bottom-line results my program could create.

Rather than try to "hard sell" the managers on the program's merits and continue to give statistical and anecdotal results that their other channel partners had received as a result of my program, I decided instead to invite two of AB Corporation's Chicago-based team members to a client's office in Chicago to observe the program in real time, with a real client.

I contacted Tom Kennedy, my client and Ambassador at SunSource in Chicago, who graciously agreed to have my prospects from AB Corporation observe our upcoming training.

While I was still setting up in the conference room, Tom greeted my guests when they arrived and proceed to tout the value of my program. When I stepped out of the conference room to welcome them, they told me Tom was already singing the praises of the program!

After observing the morning training session, during the first break of the program, my prospects from AB Corporation, Tom, and I met in a conference room to discuss the application of the one-day sales training program at AB Corporation and its channel partner XYZ Company. You can imagine my amazement when Tom continued to rave about how my program has provided value to the SunSource organization, and how it fits perfectly with the new business development initiatives that SunSource is driving home to its salespeople. Tom did such a good job "selling" the program and answering questions that I really didn't need to be in the meeting at all!

The result of bringing together this prospect, AB Corporation, with my client, SunSource, is that I may now have the opportunity not only to do training for AB Corporation's channel partner, XYZ Company, but also to be brought on as a resource for AB Corporation directly, further empowering AB Corporation as an Ambassador, which is an unbelievable opportunity.

Another client, a U.S.-based company with a large presence in Canada, also provided a great opportunity for using an Ambassador to close a deal. After working with this client for about a year in the United States conducting over a dozen sales training days for various locations, I wanted to explore the opportunity to do sales training for it in Canada.

Rather than cold calling the company's Canadian office, I decided to empower Beth, one of my Ambassadors who works for my client in the United States, to set up a conference call with the sales managers in Canada.

Luckily, she was glad to do it, and after a few conference calls listening to her promote/sell my program to her Canadian counterparts, I closed the business: five days of training for 130 reps in Canada, my largest single piece of business to date!

So, the next time you have an opportunity to close a new customer, consider your current customers who are happy with the solution or service you have provided. Take into account the type of industry, company size, annual revenue, or other relevant factors that pertain to your prospect, and match the prospect up with a current customer who has some or all of the same characteristics.

Once you find common ground between your prospect and a current customer, reach out to your current customer and ask if he or she would be willing to sit down with you and your prospect to discuss the solution you implemented for your current customer and how it was beneficial. You will find that most happy customers are more than willing to do this if you just ask.

During the meeting, after making the introductions and explaining to the prospect the solution you implemented for your current customer, watch what happens next.

As I've illustrated with my own experience using this technique, chances are, your customer will jump right in and sing your praises to your prospect, making the "close" a no-brainer.

Try this technique of empowering your current customers to do the closing for you and watch your closing ratio increase to a whole new level!

FREE TOOLS

Go to www.sittiginc.com, click on the *Power Referrals* icon, and download the "Prospects and Customer Ambassadors Pairing Worksheet" and the "ACTions to Take Worksheet."

Points to Ponder and ACTions to Take

Points to Ponder

- Introducing your prospects to happy customers creates a compelling environment for your prospects to decide to do business with you.
- When leveraging customer Ambassadors to *close* business, *you* are the one bringing the prospect and current customer together to have a discussion about the services you provide and the outstanding results you create.
- Once you find common ground between your prospect and a current customer, reach out to your current customer and ask if he or she would be willing to sit down with you and your prospect to discuss the solution you implemented for your current customer and how it was beneficial.

What I Have as Shown by the Three R's

Resources

Relationships

Reciprocity (How can I give back to my Ambassadors as it relates to this topic?)

What I Need

How I Will Get What I Need

ACTion Step 1

ACTion Step 2

ACTion Step 3

ACTion Step 4

ACTion Step 5

Index

A

W

Ward, William Arthur, 18
Websites:
    account penetration and, 54
    articles published and, 128
    blogs and, 36, 138, 141
    case studies on, 23–24
    contests and, 132
    "live" URLs in word-processed
        documents, 24
    online press and, 138–139
    press relations and, 128–131
    of publications, 140

Wilson, Woodrow, 82
Winfrey, Oprah, 18, 21
Workshops, 38–39
Writer's Market, 37
Writing:
    of case studies, 23
    to establish credibility, 25,
        36–38, 116–127, 132,
        137–138

Z

Ziglar, Zig, 15, 95, 97

About the Author

Andrea Sittig-Rolf helps sales organizations inspire change, maximize sales, and increase bottom-line results. With business savvy and a passion for people, she understands how to help salespeople be their best and to inspire them. Andrea is a successful entrepreneur, author, and sales trainer who is in high demand as a speaker and workshop leader.

Andrea is the author of two other sales books: *Business-to-Business Prospecting: Innovative Techniques to Get Your Foot in the Door with Any Prospect* (Aspatore Books, 2005) and *The Seven Keys to Effective Business-to-Business Appointment Setting: Unlock Your Sales Potential* (Aspatore Books, 2006). She is also the creator and exclusive writer of the column "Sales Solutions," formerly featured biweekly in the *Puget Sound Business Journal,* and she has been a contributing writer to SellingPower.com's "One Minute Tip," featured daily on the SellingPower.com Web site. She has been featured on several radio programs as well.

Andrea is the founder and president of Sittig Incorporated, a sales training and consulting organization based in Redmond, Washington, that has been training sales teams since May 2002. She is the developer and exclusive provider of The Blitz Experience, an activity-based sales training program that empowers salespeople to schedule appointments with qualified prospects the day of the training, resulting in a pipeline full of new opportunities at the end of the day.

In addition to her other accomplishments, Andrea is a founding author and content provider for CanDoGo, a content-rich subscription database company. CanDoGo has organized Andrea's text, voice, and video into "knowledge bytes" that have been added to its database along with content from Zig Ziglar, Dr. Denis Waitley, Tom Hopkins, Cal Ripken, Jr., Tony Parinello, and other well-known sales, motivation, and personal development leaders. For more information, please visit www.candogo.com.

Throughout her career as a sales professional, Andrea has generated millions of dollars of revenue, and she has provided inspiration to those she has trained and coached in her own sales training business. Please visit www.sittiginc.com for more information.

Sales Training Programs, Keynotes, Workshops, and Books Offered by Sittig Incorporated

Sales Training Programs

Sittig Incorporated is the creator and exclusive provider of The Blitz Experience. The Blitz Experience empowers salespeople to schedule appointments with qualified prospects the day of the training, resulting in a pipeline full of new opportunities at the end of the day. Many clients experience a 50-to–1 return on their investment based on actual sales that result from the appointments set during The Blitz Experience.

Sittig Incorporated also offers a sales training program based on Andrea's first book, *Business-to-Business Prospecting: Innovative Techniques to Get Your Foot in the Door with Any Prospect* (Aspatore, 2005). This program includes exercises and activities that reinforce the strategies and techniques presented in the book.

Keynotes

Andrea delivers informative and entertaining keynote speeches on sales-related topics at sales conferences and corporate events as well as association meetings. Choose from a variety of prepared keynotes or have one customized especially for your event. Her animated and conversational style will engage your group immediately and will keep them learning and laughing throughout the presentation.

Workshops

While Andrea's keynotes address the *why*, her workshops address the *how*. Again, you may choose from a variety of prepared workshops on various sales-related topics including Creating Power Referrals, Setting C-Level Sales Appointments, and Business-to-Business Prospecting, or you may have a workshop customized for your group. Workbooks are provided, and your team will walk away with some effective sales tools to implement on real prospects and customers long after the workshop is over.

Books

Business-to-Business Prospecting: Innovative Techniques to Get Your Foot in the Door with Any Prospect (Aspatore Books, 2005).
   The Seven Keys to Effective Business-to-Business Appointment Setting: Unlock Your Sales Potential (Aspatore Books, 2006).

*   *   *

To learn more about sales training, keynotes, and workshops, contact Sittig Incorporated at 206–769–4886 or powerreferrals@ sittiginc.com, or visit www.sittiginc.com.